prawn
cookbook

APPLE

Published by: Apple Press
Sheridan House
112/116A Western Road
Hove BN3 1DD England

© R&R Publications Marketing Pty Ltd
Project Manager: Anthony Carroll
Food Photography: Andrew Elton, Warren Webb.
Food Stylists: Stephanie Souvlis, Di Kirby
Assisting Home Economist: Jenny Fanshaw
Recipe Development: Stephanie Souvlis, Jenny Fanshaw,
Ellen Argyriou, Di Kirby
Creative Director: Vincent Wee
Design: Icon Design
Proofreader: Andrea Tarttelin

ISBN 1 84092 354 7

1. Cookery (Seafood)
641 692
First edition printed October 2000
This edition printed March 2002
Computer typeset in: Verdama, Trojan and Charcoal.
Printed in Singapore
Film Scanning by Color and Print Gallery, Malaysia

PREPARING PRAWNS

Butterflying

This is usually done on green (uncooked) prawns. It is used to increase both the visual appeal and the size of the prawns.

Cut the peeled prawn lengthwise, almost right through the flesh and along its entire length. This can be done along the stomach, which is the traditional method.
Alternatively, you can cut along the back of the prawn to give a circular shape and larger appearance.

Shelling

1. Gently twist the head and pull it from the prawns body.

2. Using your fingers, roll off the shell from the underside with the legs still attached to the shell.

3. Gently squeeze the tail and carefully remove the flesh. If you wish, the tail flap can remain attached to the body to enhance presentation.

Deveining

Using your fingers, strip the black intestinal tract (vein) out completely.

For uncooked prawns, you may need to use a small knife to make a shallow cut along the back before removing the intestinal tract.

TYPES OF PRAWNS

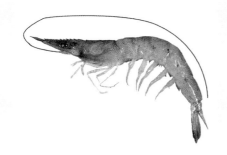

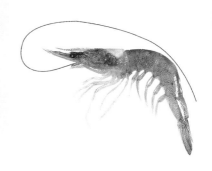

Bay Prawns

The bay prawn has a mild flavour, low oil content and relative high moisture content.

It is suited to most cookery methods – grilling, frying or barbecuing and is often used in wet dishes such as curries.

Being exceptionally sweet, it's a species that will mix beautifully with light-flavoured accompaniments. An ideal dish would be a light salad, such as the peach and prawn entrée salad.

Endeavour Prawns

They have a more distinct taste than other types of prawns, while still being low in oil and high in moisture. They are a less expensive alternative to tiger and king prawns, and their salty-sweet taste make them particularly good for use in brochette form.

School Prawns

School prawns are delicious eaten just on their own. With a mild flavour, low oiliness and high moisture content, they make excellent cocktails with a very light dressing or vinaigrette of a garlic, lemon or acid base to complement their flavour. Avoid combining strong or complex tastes with this prawn, but a hint of Thai flavours, such as a dressing of lime leaf, coriander, lemongrass and a little chilli will do it justice. Ideally suited to barbecuing and deep frying, especially shell and-all.

TYPES OF PRAWNS

Tiger Prawns

As with all other prawns, there is virtually no oil in tiger prawns, and their moderate flavour makes them ideal for grilling, barbecuing, or flambéing.

Pan- and deep-frying is also a popular way of serving these prawns. Tiger prawns are large and flavoursome and their unique red striping makes for impressive presentation. They are popular served as garlic prawns and their flavour will be enhanced by marinating in olive oil, lemon juice and lashings of garlic.

King Prawns

Are probably the most sought after prawn, and as a result can command a relatively high price. They are extremely versatile and can be used for deep-frying, barbecuing, pan-frying, and since their flavour is highly regarded, use of over-powering marinades is not necessary. On draw back on king prawns is that poor handling and storage can quickly make the flesh go tough, so extra care is needed.

Banana Prawns

Traditional cooking methods are suitable for banana prawns, but are also ideal for use in seafood dishes such as prawn cakes and crepes. They are a favourite in Asian cuisine, and their mild flavour is well suited in a marriage with spicy flavours.

Royal Red Prawns

The royal red prawn is caught way out at sea, and generally only the raw meat is available. They are considered to be good quality and makes excellent eating, especially in stir-fries and pasta sauces. The rich, sweet meat is low in fat and high in moisture.

APPROXIMATE COOKING TIMES

Cookery Method	Size	Time
Steaming	Medium-large size	10-15 minutes
	Small medium size	5-10 minutes
Boiling and Simmering	Large size	5-6 minutes/kg
	Medium size	3-4 minutes/kg
	Small size	2-3 minutes/kg
Deep-frying	Medium size	2-4 minutes
Grilling (all types)	Medium size	2-4 minutes
Microwaving	Per 125g in marinade	2 minutes

QUALITY ASSESSMENT

Test	Good Quality	Bad Quality
LOOK		
Shell condition	Clean, intact	Damaged, limp appearance
Colour	Bright, glossy	Darkening around the edges of the body segments, legs, shell, flesh, or gut areas Dry, bleached areas Faded, discoloured
Head	Firmly attached	Loose, discoloured
FEEL		
Flesh	Firm	Soft, slimy, gritty
SMELL	Mild, very slight 'prawn' odour, sea smell	Sweet 'off' smell, developing to a strong prawn smell, chemical or ammonia smell

Note: Soft and broken shells may not be an indicator of poor eating quality. The shell may be soft because the prawn has just molted.

BUYING AND STORAGE

- Green prawns are available either whole, or peeled and deveined, both fresh and frozen. Cooked prawns are available whole, shelled and deveined. For green prawns, look for a firm body with moist flesh and the shell to be tight and intact.
- Do not refreeze green prawns that have been frozen. If you plan to use prawns the night or next day after purchase, all you need to do is remove from plastic bag, place in a bowl, cover lightly and place in the coolest part of the refrigerator. If however, it will be a couple of days and you don't want to freeze them, the following are the best ways to store prawns.
- Green prawns - place in a bowl of iced water, refreshing with ice when it melts and use within 2 days.
- Cooked prawns - Place on a bowl of ice, refresh when ice melts. Don't allow to sit in water as flavours will be leeched out. Use within 2 days.
- Leave all prawns in their shell. This protects them against dehydration.
- To freeze green prawns, place them in a plastic container covered with water; do not add salt. Cover and freeze. The water forms an ice block that protects the prawns from freezer burn. To thaw, place in the refrigerator for 24 hours. You can freeze for up to 3 months.

NUTRITIONAL INFORMATION

Nutritional Information (per 100g)

Energy (kj)	Protein (g)	Fat (g)	Cholesterol (mg)	Omega 3's (mg)
371 (raw)	20.5	0.6	149	212
436(cooked)	23.5	0.9	188	n/a

SOUPS & PRAWNS

The variety of seafood soups is almost limitless; they range from is so quick, prawn and other seafood soups are among the faste

San Franciscan Seafood Chowder in a Bread Cup

INGREDIENTS

8 smallish round loaves of bread

55g/2oz butter

2 leeks, well washed & finely sliced

2 onions, finely chopped

4 cloves garlic, minced

2 carrots, peeled and chopped

1 parsnip, peeled and chopped

2 ribs celery, finely sliced

1 tablespoon fresh thyme leaves

55g/2oz plain flour

2 litres/3^{1}/2 pt fish stock

1kg/2.2 lb mixed seafood (including green prawns, mussels, clams, squid, white fish)

200mL/7fl oz thick cream

^{1}/2 bunch parsley, chopped

salt and pepper (to taste)

juice of 1 large lemon

^{1}/2 bunch of chives, chopped

METHOD

1. Preheat oven to 200 °C. First, prepare the bread bowls. Using a sharp knife, cut a large hole in the top of the bread loaf, then remove this crusty top and set aside. Carefully remove all the soft bread from the inside of the loaf leaving the surrounding crust intact.

2. Place the loaves in the preheated oven and bake for 15 minutes until the loaves are crisp and dry. Set aside.

3. Melt the butter in a large saucepan and add the chopped leeks, onions, garlic, carrots, parsnip, celery and thyme leaves. Sauté in the butter for 10 minutes until the vegetables are soft and golden. Remove the pan from the heat and sprinkle the flour over the vegetables, stirring constantly to mix the flour with the butter. Return the pan to the heat and continue stirring until the mixture begins to turn golden (about 2 minutes). This gives the flour a 'cooked' flavour.

4. Add the fish stock, stirring constantly to dissolve the roux mixture into the liquid, then simmer the soup for 20 minutes. Meanwhile, prepare the seafood by cutting the fish and shellfish into bite-sized pieces.

5. Add all the shellfish, cream, parsley and salt and pepper (to taste), and cook for a further 5 minutes. Do not allow the soup to boil rapidly because it may curdle. Once the shellfish has cooked, stir the lemon juice through the fish and ladle the soup into the bread bowls. Garnish with a some chopped chives and serve.

Serves 8

bisques to substantial bouillabaisses. As the cooking time for prawns
soups to prepare, making them ideal for last-minute entertaining.

Hot and Sour Prawn Soup

INGREDIENTS

1kg/2.2lb medium uncooked prawns

1 tablespoon vegetable oil

8 slices fresh or bottled galangal or fresh
  ginger

8 kaffir lime leaves

2 stalks fresh lemon grass, bruised, or

1 teaspoon dried lemon grass, soaked in hot
  water until soft

2 fresh red chillies, halved and seeded

2 litres/3^1/$_2$ pt water

3 tablespoons fresh coriander (cilantro)
  leaves

1 fresh red chilli, chopped

2 tablespoons lime juice

shredded kaffir lime leaf

METHOD

1. Shell prawns and devein. Reserve heads
and shells. Heat oil in a large saucepan over
a high heat, add prawn heads and shells and
cook, stirring, for 5 minutes or until shells
change colour. Stir in galangal or ginger, lime
leaves, lemon grass, halved chillies and
water, cover and bring to simmering.
Simmer, stirring occasionally, for 15 minutes.

2. Strain liquid into a clean saucepan and
discard solids. Add prawns and cook for 2
minutes. Stir in coriander (cilantro), chopped
chilli and lime juice and cook for 1 minute or
until prawns are tender.

3. Ladle soup into bowls and garnish with
shredded lime leaves.

Serves 4

Prawn and Chicken Soup

INGREDIENTS

1 tablespoon vegetable oil

1 onion, diced

1 red capsicum (pepper), diced

2 cloves garlic, crushed

1 teaspoon finely chopped fresh ginger

1 litre/1^3/$_4$ pt chicken stock

115g/4oz boneless chicken thigh or
  breast, fillets, sliced

20 uncooked small prawns, shelled and
  deveined

115g/4oz rice noodles

115g/4oz canned bamboo shoots,
  drained and sliced

5 button mushrooms, thinly sliced

^{1}/$_4$ lettuce, shredded

2 spring onions, thinly sliced

2 tablespoons finely chopped fresh
  coriander

1^1/$_2$ tablespoons soy sauce

freshly ground black pepper

METHOD

1. Heat oil in a saucepan over a
medium heat, add onion and red capsicum
(pepper) and cook, stirring, for 5 minutes or
until onion is soft. Add garlic and ginger and
cook for 2 minutes longer.

2. Stir in stock and bring to the boil. Add
chicken, prawns, noodles, bamboo shoots
and mushrooms, reduce heat and simmer for
5 minutes or until noodles are tender.

3. Stir in lettuce, spring onions, coriander,
soy sauce and black pepper to taste and
serve immediately.

Serves 4

ot and Sour Prawn Soup

Prawn and Chicken Soup

SOUPS

1

American Shrimp Bisque

INGREDIENTS

85g/3oz butter

3 tablespoon finely chopped onion

1 stalk celery, finely chopped

1 tablespoon plain flour

1kg/2lb cooked prawns, shelled, deveined
   and chopped

875mL/$1^1/_2$ pt warm milk

115mL/4fl oz double cream

2 tablespoons sherry

salt

freshly ground black pepper

paprika

freshly grated nutmeg

3 tablespoon chopped fresh
parsley or snipped chives

METHOD

1. Melt butter in a saucepan over low heat,
add onion and celery, cover and cook for 5
minutes, taking care not to let vegetables
brown.

2. Stir in flour and cook for 1 minute. Add
prawns. Gradually stir in milk until blended.
Bring to the boil, lower heat and cook,
stirring, for 2 minutes or until soup thickens.

Stir in cream and heat through without
boiling.

3. Stir sherry into soup and season to taste
with salt, black pepper, paprika and nutmeg.
Garnish servings with parsley.

Serves 4

Prawn Bisque

INGREDIENTS

315g/11oz cooked prawns, shelled and
   deveined

$^1/_2$ onion, diced

$^1/_2$ cup/115mL/4fl oz tomato paste
   (purée)

600mL/1pt chicken stock

85mL/3fl oz cream (double)

$^1/_4$ teaspoon paprika

freshly ground black pepper

1-2 tablespoons dry sherry

METHOD

1. Place prawns, onion and tomato
paste (purée) in a food processor or
blender and process to make a purée.
With machine running, slowly add stock
and process to combine.

2. Place prawn mixture in a saucepan
and cook over a low heat, stirring
frequently, for 10 minutes or until the
mixture comes to the boil.

3. Stir in cream, paprika and black
pepper to taste and cook for 2 minutes
or until heated through. Stir in sherry
and serve immediately.

Serves 6

anhattan restaurants. Offer small crackers or wafer biscuits on the side.

Spanish Fish Soup with Saffron

INGREDIENTS

2 tablespoons olive oil

2 large carrots, finely chopped

3 leeks, finely sliced and well washed

1 red capsicum (pepper), chopped

1 green capsicum (pepper), chopped

1 tablespoon Spanish paprika

large pinch of saffron threads

2 cups/450mL/16fl oz white wine

3 cups/675mL/24fl oz fish stock

400g/14oz firm white fish fillets

400g/14oz prawns, shelled and deveined

400g/14oz baby calamari or squid

2 tablespoons chopped parsley

1 lemon, cut into wedges

METHOD

1. Heat the olive oil in a large saucepan and add the carrots, leeks and capsicums (peppers) and sauté until softened, (about 10 minutes) Add the paprika and saffron, continuing to cook for a few minutes more.

2. Add the wine and stock and bring the soup to the boil, simmering for 15 minutes. Add the diced fish, shelled prawns and squid and simmer for a further 5 minutes.

Serves 6

INGREDIENTS

4 cups/1 litre/1³/₄ pt fish stock
5 cm/2 in piece fresh galangal, sliced
 or 8 pieces dried galangal
8 kaffir lime leaves
2 stalks fresh lemon grass, finely
 chopped or 1 teaspoon dried lemon
 grass, soaked in hot water until soft
2 tablespoons lime juice
2 tablespoons finely sliced lime rind
2 tablespoons Thai fish sauce (nam pla)
2 tablespoons Thai Red Curry Paste
500g/1 lb uncooked large prawns,
shelled and deveined, tails left intact
3 spring onions, sliced diagonally
3 tablespoons fresh coriander (cilantro)
 leaves
1 small fresh red chilli, sliced

Method

1. Place stock in large saucepan and bring to the boil over a medium heat, add galangal, lime leaves, lemon grass, lime juice, lime rind, fish sauce and curry paste and simmer, stirring occasionally, for 10 minutes.

2. Add prawns and spring onions and simmer for 5 minutes longer or until prawns are cooked.

3. Remove galangal and discard. Sprinkle soup with coriander (cilantro) leaves and sliced chilli and serve.

Serves 4

Chunky Corn and Prawn Gazpacho

INGREDIENTS

4 large Roma tomatoes, washed and
  halved
1 yellow capsicum (pepper), seeded
  and quartered
$^1/_4$-$^1/_2$ teaspoon Tabasco sauce
1 teaspoon salt, or to taste
2 ears of corn
1 small leek, white parts only
1 clove garlic, peeled
1 small Spanish onion
1 tablespoon olive oil
2 teaspoons mild, sweet paprika
500g/1 lb shelled raw king prawns,
  tails on
juice of two limes
2 tablespoons chopped fresh parsley
handful fresh coriander (cilantro)
  leaves, chopped
lime wedges, to serve

Method

1. First, make the spicy sauce. Process the tomatoes in a food processor briefly then pour the mixture into a large bowl. Process the yellow capsicum (pepper) pieces until finely chopped and add these to the tomatoes. Add Tabasco sauce and salt to taste. Set aside in the fridge for an hour or up to eight hours.

2. Using a sharp knife, cut the corn off the ears. Heat a heavy frypan over a high heat then add the corn and 'dry fry' the corn until it is slightly charred and golden brown. Pour into a small bowl and set aside.

3. Wash the leek thoroughly then place the white parts only, the garlic and the Spanish onion in a food processor and chop finely. Alternatively, chop finely with a knife. To the frypan, add the oil and heat, then add the finely chopped leek, Spanish onion, garlic mixture and the paprika and sauté over a medium heat for 5 minutes until the vegetables have softened and begun to turn gold around the edges of the pan.

4. Move the onions to the side of the pan and add the peeled raw prawns. Allow the prawns to cook for a moment or two until they are orange in colour underneath then turn them over and cook the other side.

5. Bring the onions in from the side of the pan and toss with the prawns. Add the prawn mixture to the chilled tomato mixture and toss thoroughly. Add half of the charred corn and the lime juice and parsley and mix well before returning to the fridge to chill.

6. To serve, divide the mixture between 6 martini glasses or wine goblets and top with coriander (cilantro) leaves and remaining charred corn.

Serves 6

CHUNKY CORN AND
PRAWN GAZPACHO

Tom Yam Gong

INGREDIENTS

3 cups/675mL/24fl oz fish stock
1 tablespoon chopped fresh lemon
  grass or 1 teaspoon dried lemon grass
$1/2$ teaspoon finely grated lemon rind
2 tablespoons Thai fish sauce
225g/8oz button mushrooms, sliced
500g/1lb large uncooked prawns,
  shelled and deveined
85mL/3fl oz cream (double)
115g/4oz bean sprouts
2 spring onions, cut into 2cm/$3/4$ in
  lengths
1 teaspoon chilli paste (sambal oelek)
85mL/3fl oz lemon juice
3 tablespoons chopped fresh coriander
  (cilantro)
freshly ground black pepper

METHOD

1. Place stock in a large saucepan and
bring to the boil. Stir in lemon grass,
lemon rind, fish sauce, mushrooms and
prawns and cook for 3-4 minutes or until
prawns change colour.

2. Reduce heat to low, stir in cream and
cook for 2-3 minutes or until heated
through.

3. Remove pan from heat, add bean
sprouts, spring onions, chilli paste (sambal
oelek), lemon juice, coriander and black
pepper to taste. Serve immediately.

Serves 4

Bouillabaisse

INGREDIENTS

3kg/6^{1}/2 lb mixed fish and seafood,
  including firm white fish fillets, prawns,
  mussels, crab and calamari (squid) rings
^{1}/4 cup/55mL/2fl oz olive oil
2 cloves garlic, crushed
2 large onions, chopped
2 leeks, sliced
2 x 440g/15^{1}/2oz canned tomatoes,
  undrained and mashed
1 tablespoon chopped fresh thyme or 1
  teaspoon dried thyme
2 tablespoons chopped fresh basil or 1^{1}/2
  teaspoons dried basil
2 tablespoons chopped fresh parsley
2 bay leaves
2 tablespoons finely grated orange rind
1 teaspoon saffron threads
1 cup/225mL/8fl oz dry white wine
1 cup/225mL/8fl oz fish stock
freshly ground black pepper

Method

1. Remove bones and skin from fish fillets
and cut into 2 cm/^{3}/4 in cubes. Peel and
devein prawns, leaving tails intact. Scrub and
remove beards from mussels. Cut crab into
quarters. Set aside.

2. Heat oil in a large saucepan over a
medium heat, add garlic, onions and leeks
and cook for 5 minutes or until onions are
golden. Add tomatoes, thyme, basil, parsley,
bay leaves, orange rind, saffron, wine and
stock and bring to the boil. Reduce heat and
simmer for 30 minutes.

3. Add fish and crab and cook for 10
minutes, add remaining and cook for 5
minutes longer or until fish and seafood are
cooked. Season to taste with black pepper.

Serves 6

Prawn and Crab Soup

INGREDIENTS

6 tomatoes, chopped
2 onions, chopped
1 tablespoon vegetable oil
4 cloves garlic, crushed
1 tablespoon oregano leaves
2 fresh coriander (cilantro) plants
1 fish head, such snapper, perch,
   cod or haddock
$2^1/2$ litres/$4^1/4$ pt water
2 uncooked crabs, cleaned and cut
   into serving pieces
12 medium uncooked prawns, shelled
   and deveined
185g/$6^1/2$oz fish fillet, cut into chunks

METHOD

1. Place tomatoes and onions in a food processor or blender and process to make a purée.

2. Heat oil in a saucepan over medium heat, add garlic and cook, stirring, for 1 minute or until golden. Stir in tomato mixture, then add oregano leaves and coriander (cilantro) plants, bring to simmering and simmer for 15 minutes. Add fish head and water and simmer 20 minutes. Strain stock and discard solids. Return stock to a clean saucepan.

3. Add crabs and prawns to stock, bring to simmering and simmer for 3 minutes. Add fish and simmer for 1-2 minutes or until all the seafood is cooked.

Serves 6

Prawn and Wonton Soup

INGREDIENTS

$2^1/2$ litres/4 pt chicken stock
1 carrot, cut into thin strips
1 stalk celery, cut into thin strips
$1/2$ red capsicum (pepper), cut into thin
   strips
24 large cooked prawns, shelled
   and deveined

Pork Wontons

225g/8oz pork mince
1 egg, lightly beaten
2 spring onions, chopped
1 fresh red chilli, seeded and chopped
1 tablespoon soy sauce
1 tablespoon oyster sauce
24 spring roll or wonton wrappers,
   each $12^1/2$ cm/5 in square

METHOD

1. To make wontons, place pork, egg, spring onions, chilli, soy sauce and oyster sauce in a bowl and mix to combine.

2. Place spoonfuls of mixture in the centre of each spring roll or wonton wrapper, then draw the corners together and twist to form small bundles. Place wontons in a steamer set over a saucepan of boiling water and steam for 3-4 minutes or until wontons are cooked.

3. Place chicken stock in a saucepan and bring to the boil over a medium heat. Add carrot, celery and red capsicum (pepper) and simmer for 1 minute. Add prawns and cook for 1 minute longer.

4. To serve, place 3-4 wontons in each soup bowl and carefully ladle over soup. Serve immediately.

Serves 6-8

SALADS & STARTERS

As a main meal or as a starter, a prawn salad is always we **avocado and prawn salad, peach and prawn entrée salad a** **sure that it will not only taste good but it will also be goo**

Peach and Prawn Entrée Salad

INGREDIENTS
200g/7oz dried peaches
1 tablespoon lemon juice
2 teaspoons lemon zest, grated
2 teaspoons brown sugar
$1/2$ teaspoon salt
$1/2$ teaspoon freshly ground black pepper
$1/3$ cup/75mL/2^1/2fl oz sherry vinegar
2 drops Tabasco sauce
500g/1.1lb salad mix
2 teaspoon Dijon mustard
1 egg
$2/3$ cup/150mL/5^1/4fl oz light olive oil
12 king prawns, shelled and deveined

METHOD
1. Place dried peaches in a flat dish. Mix next 7 ingredients together and pour over the peaches. Allow to stand at room temperature for 30 minutes.

2. Remove peaches from vinegar mixture. Pour the vinegar mixture into a blender or food processor, add the mustard and egg, and process until smooth. With the motor running, add the oil in a thin, steady stream. Dressing will become creamy and thicken slightly.

3. Divide salad mix between 4 plates and place 2 peach halves on slope of salad and arrange 3 prawns on each plate. Spoon dressing over the salad and serve immediately.

Serves 4

2

. In this chapter you will find exciting recipes for salads, such as couscous salad with seafood. Whichever one you choose, you can be ou.

Prawn and Avocado Salad

INGREDIENTS

750g/1^1/2 lb cooked king prawns
1 avocado, sliced
1 grapefruit, segmented
Dressing
2 tablespoons mayonnaise
2 tablespoons sour cream
1 tablespoon yoghurt
2 tablespoons chopped mint

METHOD

1. Shelled and devein prawns.

2. Arrange prawns, avocado and grapefruit on a serving plate. Drizzle with combined mayonnaise, sour cream, yoghurt and mint.

Serves 4

Mediterranean Salad

INGREDIENTS

185g/6^1/2oz couscous
2 cups/450mL/16fl oz boiling water
1 tablespoon olive oil
1 tablespoon balsamic vinegar
freshly ground black pepper
1 cucumber, sliced
1 green capsicum (pepper), chopped
3 plum (egg or Italian) tomatoes, chopped
12 sun-dried tomatoes, sliced
55g/2oz marinated artichokes, drained
 and sliced
55g/2oz pitted black olives, sliced
185g/6^1/2oz cooked prawns, shelled and
 deveined (optional)
115g/4oz feta cheese, cut into
 2cm/^{3}/4 in cubes
2 tablespoons chopped fresh basil or
2 teaspoons dried basil
2 teaspoons finely grated lime or
 lemon rind

METHOD

1. Place couscous in a bowl, pour over boiling water and toss with a fork until couscous absorbs all the liquid. Add oil, vinegar and black pepper to taste and toss to combine. Set aside.

2. Place cucumber, green capsicum (pepper), fresh and dried tomatoes, artichokes, olives, prawns (if using), feta cheese, basil and lime or lemon rind in a salad bowl and toss to combine. Add couscous mixture and toss.

Serves 4

rawn and Avocado Salad

Mediterranean Salad

Tomato, Corn and Prawn Salad

INGREDIENTS

2 cups/300g/10^{1}/$_{2}$oz cooked corn kernels

1 onion, finely sliced

200g/7oz shelled, deveined cooked prawns, cut into 1cm/^{1}/$_{2}$ in lengths

2 tomatoes, chopped

55g/2oz spring onions, chopped

1 red capsicum (peppers), seeded and finely chopped

2 tablespoons red wine vinegar

2 tablespoons olive oil

1 clove garlic, crushed

1 tablespoon fresh lemon juice

METHOD

1. In a large bowl, combine the corn, onion, prawns, tomato, spring onions and capsicum (pepper), mix well.

2. Mix together the vinegar, oil, garlic and lemon juice and toss through salad.

Serves 4

Avocado Seafood

INGREDIENTS

6 baby octopus
500g/1 lb school prawns
3 ripe avocados
<u>**Dressing**</u>
$1/3$ cup/75mL/$2^1/2$ fl oz olive oil
2 tablespoons lemon juice
1 hard boiled egg, finely chopped
1 tablespoon fresh oregano, chopped
2 cloves garlic, crushed

METHOD

1. Remove heads from octopus just below eye level. Wash well. Drop octopus into simmering water, cook until just opaque, drain, rinse under cold water. Cut octopus into bite size pieces. Combine with dressing. Marinate in refrigerator overnight.

2. Peel and devein prawns, stir into octopus. Halve avocados, remove seeds. Pile seafood on top of avocado halves, garnish with lemon and oregano.

Serves 6

Couscous Salad with Seafood and Fresh Mint

INGREDIENTS

$^1/_2$ cup/115mL/4fl oz olive oil

55mL/2fl oz fresh lemon juice

1 large clove garlic, minced

1 teaspoon celery seed

salt and pepper to taste

$^1/_4$ teaspoon turmeric

$^1/_4$ teaspoon cumin

400mL/14fl oz boiling vegetable stock

500g/1 lb green king prawns, shelled, tail
 left on

200g/7oz small calamari rings

300g/10$^1/_2$oz couscous

3 tomatoes, finely diced

2 stalks celery, finely sliced

6 spring onions, chopped

20 fresh mint leaves, finely sliced

METHOD

1. Whisk together olive oil, lemon juice, garlic and celery seed until thick then season with salt and pepper. Set aside.

2. Add turmeric and cumin to the simmering stock and stir. Add the prawns and calamari and poach gently for 2 minutes or until the prawns are orange then remove from the stock.

3. Place the couscous in a large bowl then pour the remaining spiced stock over. Stir well and cover then allow to stand until water is absorbed, about 10 minutes.

4. Fluff up with a fork and add prawn and calamari mixture, diced tomatoes, celery, spring onions and mint. Add dressing and mix well.

Serves 6

Sri Lankan Prawn Salad

INGREDIENTS

1 kg/2lb large cooked prawns, shelled
 and deveined

1 grapefruit, segmented

1 orange, segmented

2 bananas, peeled and sliced

1 onion, sliced

6 spinach leaves, shredded

30g/1oz cashews, chopped

Dressing

2 tablespoons lemon juice

225g/8oz natural yoghurt

1 teaspoon curry powder

2 tablespoons mayonnaise

METHOD

1. To make dressing, place lemon juice, yoghurt, curry powder and mayonnaise in a bowl and mix to combine.

2. Place prawns, grapefruit, orange, bananas, onion and spinach in a salad bowl. Spoon dressing over salad and toss. Sprinkle over cashews. Cover and chill.

Serves 6

Couscous Salad with Seafood and Fresh Mint

Prawn, Avocado and Mango Salad

Prawn, Avocado and Mango Salad

INGREDIENTS

32 cooked medium prawns, peeled, tails
  intact
2 medium mangoes, cut into thin strips
1 large avocado, flesh cut into thin strips
2 tablespoons finely grated lime rind
1/2 teaspoon fresh chilli, very finely chopped
1/4 teaspoon cracked black pepper
2 tablespoon freshly squeezed lemon juice
3 tablespoons olive oil
1 bunch dill

METHOD

1. Decoratively arrange the prawns, mango slices and avocado on a serving plate.

2. Combine the lime rind, chilli, pepper, lemon juice and olive oil, mix well and pour over salad. Garnish with sprigs of fresh dill.

Serves 4

Prawn and Green Bean Salad with Dill Sauce

INGREDIENTS

1 1/2kg/3lb uncooked prawns
115g/4oz green beans, topped and
  tailed
2 sticks celery, thinly sliced
6 spring onions, sliced
3 tablespoons chopped fresh parsley
lemon juice
4 hard-boiled eggs, roughly chopped
Dill Sauce
115mL/4fl oz natural low fat yoghurt
115mL/4fl oz reduced fat mayonnaise
3 tablespoons chopped fresh dill
freshly squeezed juice of 1/2 lemon
salt

METHOD

1. Bring a large saucepan of salted water to the boil, add prawns, cook until prawns change colour (about 3 minutes). Drain and rinse under cold running water. Peel and devein prawns.

2. Plunge green beans in boiling water, allow water to return to boil, drain beans immediately. Refresh under cold running water and drain thoroughly.

3. Combine beans, celery, prawns, spring onions and parsley in a salad bowl, sprinkle with lemon juice, toss well to mix. Cover and refrigerate until ready to serve.

4. To make Dill Sauce: Combine yoghurt, mayonnaise, dill and lemon juice in a small bowl, whisk vigorously until well blended. Season to taste with salt.

5. Serve salad cold or at room temperature with sauce in a separate bowl. Add chopped eggs to salad after the sauce is added.

Serves 4

Prawr

Scallop and Prawn Salad

INGREDIENTS

12 uncooked king prawns, shelled and
   deveined
500g/1 lb scallops
2 large onions, sliced

Dressing

2 teaspoons finely chopped fresh dill
2 teaspoons finely chopped fresh parsley
2 teaspoons finely chopped fresh chives
1 cloves garlic, crushed
1 tablespoons lime juice
115mL/4fl oz red wine vinegar
4 tablespoons vegetable oil
freshly ground black pepper

METHOD

1. Heat up fry pan or barbecue hotplate and
cook scallops, prawns and onions for 3-4
minutes.Allow to cool

2. Combine all ingredients for dressing, and
mix well.

3. Place seafood and onion in a bowl and toss
in the dressing.

Serves 6

Prawn and Pawpaw Salad

INGREDIENTS

2 teaspoons vegetable oil

2 teaspoons chilli paste (sambal oelek)

2 stalks fresh lemon grass, chopped, or 1 teaspoon
dried lemon grass, soaked in hot water until soft

2 tablespoons shredded fresh ginger

500g/1lb medium uncooked prawns, shelled and
deveined

$^1/_2$ Chinese cabbage, shredded

4 red or golden shallots, chopped

1 pawpaw, peeled and sliced

55g/2oz watercress leaves

55g/2oz chopped roasted peanuts

30g/1oz fresh coriander (cilantro) leaves

LIME AND COCONUT DRESSING

1 teaspoon brown sugar

3 tablespoons lime juice

2 tablespoons Thai fish sauce (nam pla)

1 tablespoon coconut vinegar

METHOD

1. Heat oil in a frying pan over a high heat, add
chilli paste (sambal oelek), lemon grass and
ginger and stir-fry for 1 minute. Add prawns and
stir-fry for 2 minutes or until prawns change
colour and are cooked through. Set aside to cool.

2. Arrange cabbage, shallots, pawpaw,
watercress, peanuts, coriander (cilantro) and
prawn mixture attractively on a serving platter.

3. To make dressing, place sugar, lime juice, fish
sauce and vinegar in a bowl and mix to combine.
Drizzle dressing over salad and serve.

Serves 4

Seafood Salad

INGREDIENTS

375g/13^1/4oz calamari (squid) rings
1 tablespoon olive oil
375g/13^1/4oz uncooked medium prawns,
  peeled and deveined
1 clove garlic, crushed
1 bunch/500g/1 lb English spinach
1 red onion, sliced
1 red capsicum (pepper), cut into strips
225g/8oz snow peas (mangetout),
  trimmed
2 tablespoons fresh mint leaves
30g/1oz nuts, finely chopped

CHILLI DRESSING

2 tablespoons sweet chilli sauce
1 tablespoon soy sauce
1 tablespoon lime juice
1 tablespoon vegetable oil

METHOD

1. Place calamari (squid) on absorbent kitchen paper and pat dry.

2. Heat oil in a frying pan over a medium heat, add prawns and garlic and stir-fry for 2 minutes. Add squid (calamari) and stir-fry for 2 minutes longer. Set aside to cool.

3. Arrange spinach leaves, onion, red pepper, snow peas (mangetout), mint and nuts in a bowl or on a serving platter. Top with seafood mixture.

4. To make dressing, place chilli sauce, soy sauce, lime juice and oil in a bowl and mix to combine. Spoon dressing over salad and chill.

Serving suggestion: This dish only requires fresh crusty bread or rolls.

Serves 4

Seafood and Vegetable Salad

INGREDIENTS

2 cups/440g/15^1/2oz long grain rice,
  cooked
225g/8oz cooked prawns, shelled and
  deveined
225g/8oz canned crab meat, drained and
  flaked
115g/4oz boneless white fish fillet, thinly
  sliced (optional)
85g/3oz button mushrooms, sliced
6 spring onions, sliced
1 carrot, thinly sliced
30g/1 oz sliced green beans
1 egg omelette, thinly sliced

Rice Vinegar Dressing

^{1}/2 cup/125mL/4fl oz rice vinegar
2 tablespoons mirin
1 tablespoon soy sauce
1 tablespoon sugar

METHOD

1. Place rice, prawns, crab meat, fish (if using) mushrooms, spring onions, carrot and beans in a large salad bowl and toss to combine.

2. To make dressing, place rice vinegar, mirin, soy sauce and sugar in a bowl and whisk to combine. Drizzle dressing over salad, cover and refrigerate. Just prior to serving, top with omelette strips.

Serves 6

SEAFOOD SALAD

2

Prawn and Pineapple Salad

INGREDIENTS

1 tablespoon fresh lemon juice
2 tablespoons white wine vinegar
1 tablespoon dijon mustard
$^1/_4$ cup/55mL/2fl oz olive oil
2 tablepoons oriental sesame oil
10 water chestnuts, drained and chopped
1 tablespoon grated green ginger
225g/8oz can sliced pineapple, drained
  and cut into chunks
500g/1lb cooked prawns, shelled
  lettuce for serving
3 spring onions, sliced
1 tablespoon sesame seeds, toasted lightly

METHOD

1. To make dressing, whisk the lemon juice, vinegar and mustard together then gradually add the oils, whisking all the time until dressing is thickened.

2. In a bowl add the chopped water chestnuts, ginger, pineapple and prawns. Add the dressing and toss together lightly.

3. Arrange the salad on lettuce cups and garnish with spring onion and sesame seeds.

Serves 4

Prawn and White Bean Salad

INGREDIENTS

3 x 315g/11oz canned cannellini beans,
  rinsed and drained
185g/6$^1/_2$oz celery, thinly sliced
1 small red onion, thinly sliced
6 tablespoon olive oil
3 cloves garlic, chopped
$^1/_2$ teaspoon dried hot red pepper flakes
750g/1$^1/_2$lb prawns, shelled and
  deveined
55mL/2fl oz lemon juice, or to taste
3 tablespoons chopped fresh parsley
1 tablespoon finely chopped fresh oregano
or 1 teaspoon dried oregano
8 lettuce leaves

METHOD

1. Place drained beans, celery and onion in a bowl and lightly mix to combine. Heat half the oil in a large heavy frying pan and cook garlic and red pepper flakes for 30 seconds or until fragrant. Add prawns and cook, stirring, for 2-3 minutes or until just tender.

2. Add prawn mixture to beans with lemon juice, remaining oil, herbs, salt and black pepper to taste and toss well. Cover and chill until served.

3. At the picnic, arrange 2 lettuce leaves on each plate and top with salad.

Serves 4

Prawn and Snowpea (Mangetout) Salad with Sweet Chilli Sauce

INGREDIENTS

3/4cup/170mL/6fl oz sweet white wine

1 tablespoon freshly squeezed lemon juice

1 tablespoon freshly squeezed lime juice

1 teaspoon sugar

1 teaspoon sambal oelek (chilli paste)

1 teaspoon cracked black pepper

1/2 teaspoon ground coriander

300g/10^1/2oz scallops

300g/10^1/2oz green king prawns, shelled, deveined and tail intact

75g/2^1/2 oz snowpeas (mangetout)

2 tablespoons oil

1 tablespoon chopped parsley

METHOD

1. Heat the wine, lemon juice, lime juice, sugar, chilli paste, pepper and coriander in a large frying pan over moderate heat until boiling.

2. Reduce heat, simmer, add scallops and prawns, cook for 2 minutes or until cooked through. Remove and set aside.

3. Add snowpeas to the frying pan, cook for 30 seconds, remove with slotted spoon and add to the prawns and scallops.

4. Add the oil and parsley to the pan juices, cook for 1 minute, then pour over scallops, prawns and snowpeas. Toss well and chill until ready to serve.

Serves 4

OUTDOOR PRAWNS

Whether it's a special celebration or just a few friends around for a b

cooking times, prawns are perfect for barbecuing. This imaginative s

Barbecued Marinated Prawns

INGREDIENTS

1kg/2lb uncooked medium prawns, shelled
  and deveined, tails left intact
<u>Chilli and Herb Marinade</u>
2 fresh red chillies, chopped
2 cloves garlic, crushed
1 tablespoon chopped fresh oregano
1 tablespoon chopped fresh parsley
1/4 cup/55mL/2fl oz olive oil
2 tablespoons balsamic vinegar
freshly ground black pepper

METHOD

1. Preheat barbecue to a medium heat.

2. To make marinade, place chillies, garlic, oregano, parsley, oil, vinegar and black pepper to taste in a bowl and mix to combine.

Add prawns, toss to coat and marinate for 10 minutes.

3. Drain prawns and cook on oiled barbecue for 1-2 minutes each side or until prawns just change colour.
Serves 8

Hot Chilli Prawns

INGREDIENTS

1 1/2 kg/3lb uncooked large prawns,
  peeled and deveined with tails left
  intact
<u>Chilli Marinade</u>
2 teaspoons cracked black pepper
2 tablespoons sweet chilli sauce
1 tablespoon soy sauce
1 clove garlic, crushed
1/4 cup/55mL/2fl oz lemon juice

<u>Mango Cream</u>
1 mango, peeled, stoned and roughly
  chopped
3 tablespoons coconut milk

METHOD

1. To make marinade, place black pepper, chilli sauce, soy sauce, garlic and lemon juice in a bowl and mix to combine.
Add prawns, toss to coat, cover and set aside to marinate for 1 hour. Toss several times during marinating.

2. To make Mango Cream, place mango flesh and coconut milk in a food processor or blender and process until smooth.

3. Preheat barbecue to a medium heat. Drain prawns and cook on lightly oiled barbecue for 3-4 minutes or until prawns change colour. Serve immediately with Mango Cream.

Coconut milk: This can be purchased in a number of forms: canned, as a long-life product in cartons, or as a powder to which you add water. Once opened it has a short life and should be used within a day or so. It is available from Asian food stores and some supermarkets, however if you have trouble finding it you can easily make your own. To make coconut milk, place 500g/1 lb desiccated coconut in a bowl and add 750mL/1 1/2 pt of boiling water. Set aside to stand for 30 minutes, then strain, squeezing the coconut to extract as much liquid as possible. This will make a thick coconut milk. The coconut can be used again to make a weaker coconut milk.
Serves 6

3

...eat and a chat, barbecuing is a wonderful way to entertain. With their quick
...n of dishes will have you serving these water creatures from the barbecue regularly.

Hot Chilli Prawns

Seafood Paella

INGREDIENTS

1 tablespoon olive oil

2 onions, chopped

2 cloves garlic, crushed

1 tablespoon fresh thyme leaves

2 teaspoons finely grated lemon rind

4 ripe tomatoes, chopped

2^1/$_2$ cups/500g/1 lb short grain white rice

pinch saffron threads soaked in

2 cups/450mL/16 fl oz water

1^1/$_5$ litres/2 pt chicken or fish stock

315g/11oz fresh or frozen peas

2 red capsicums (peppers), chopped

1kg/2 lb mussels, scrubbed and
  beards removed

500g/1 lb firm white fish fillets, chopped

315g/11oz peeled uncooked prawns

200g/7oz scallops

3 squid (calamari) tubes, sliced

1 tablespoon chopped fresh parsley

METHOD

1. Preheat barbecue to a medium heat. Place a large paella or frying pan on barbecue, add oil and heat. Add onions, garlic, thyme leaves and lemon rind and cook for 3 minutes or until onion is soft.

2. Add tomatoes and cook, stirring, for 4 minutes. Add rice and cook, stirring, for 4 minutes longer or until rice is translucent. Stir in saffron mixture and stock and bring to simmering. Simmer, stirring occasionally, for 30 minutes or until rice has absorbed almost all of the liquid.

3. Stir in peas, red capsicum (peppers) and mussels and cook for 2 minutes. Add fish, prawns and scallops and cook, stirring, for 2-3 minutes. Stir in squid (calamari) and parsley and cook, stirring, for 1-2 minutes longer or until seafood is cooked.

Serves 8

Marinated Prawns Wrapped in Bacon

INGREDIENTS

32 green king prawns, peeled and deveined
$^1/_4$ cup/55mL/2fl oz fresh lime juice
1 clove garlic, crushed
1 tablespoon grated ginger
2 tablespoons brown sugar
16 bacon rashers, rind removed

METHOD

1. Place prawns in a medium bowl with the lime juice, garlic, ginger and sugar, mix well. Cover and refrigerate for 30 minutes.

2. Cut bacon into strips, about 2$^1/_2$cm/1 in wide and wrap around each prawn. Thread two prawns onto each skewer.

3. Grill under a moderate heat for 2 minutes each side or until cooked through.

Served 4

Scallop and Prawn Sticks

INGREDIENTS
6 uncooked king prawns, shelled and deveined
500g/1 lb scallops
1 large onion, cut into eighths

<u>Marinade</u>
1 tablespoon olive oil
2 tablespoons white wine
2 teaspoons finely chopped fresh dill
2 teaspoons finely chopped fresh parsley
2 teaspoons finely chopped fresh chives
2 cloves garlic, crushed
2 teaspoons grated lime rind
2 tablespoons lime juice
freshly ground black pepper

METHOD
1. Thread prawns, scallops and onions onto six wooden skewers.

2. To make marinade, combine oil, wine, dill, parsley, chives, garlic, lime rind and juice in a glass dish. Season to taste with pepper. Add skewered seafood and marinate for 1 hour.

3. Remove seafood from marinade and grill for 2–3 minutes each side, turning and brushing with marinade frequently.

Serves 6

ADD AN EXOTIC TOUCH TO YOUR
NEXT BARBECUE WITH
THESE EASY TO PREPARE AND
TASTY KEBABS.

Sesame Barbecued Prawns

INGREDIENTS

1kg/2 lb medium-large king prawns
65mL/2fl oz olive oil
65mL/2fl oz red wine
4 shallots, finely chopped
1 teaspoon, grated lemon rind
$^1/_2$ teaspoon cracked black pepper
12 bamboo skewers (soaked in water for 30 minutes)
115g/4oz toasted sesame seeds

METHOD

1. Peel and devein prawns (leaving the shell tails intact).

2. Combine oil, wine, shallots, lemon rind and pepper, mix well.

3. Thread the prawns onto bamboo skewers (approximately 3 per skewer).

4. Place the skewers in a shallow dish and pour marinade over. Allow to marinate for at least 1 hour.

5. Roll the prawns in the toasted sesame seeds, pressing them on well. Refrigerate for 30 minutes before cooking.

6. Cook on the hotplate of a well-heated barbecue for 2 minutes each side.

7. Brush with marinade during cooking.

Serves 6–8

Vietnamese Barbecue Prawns

INGREDIENTS

500g/1 lb large green prawns
185g/6oz thin vermicelli
 boiling water
2 teaspoons vegetable oil
6 green shallots, chopped
$^1/_2$ cup/ 75g/2$^1/_2$ oz roasted peanuts
$^1/_2$ bunch coriander (cilantro) leaves,
 chopped

<u>Nuoc Cham Sauce</u>
2 garlic cloves, peeled
2 dried red chillies
5 teaspoons sugar
juice and pulp of $^1/_2$ limes
4 tablespoons fish sauce
5 tablespoons water

METHOD

1. To make sauce, pound garlic, chillies and sugar using a pestle and mortar. Add lime juice and pulp, then the fish sauce and water. Mix well to combine the ingredients.

2. Slit prawns down back, remove vein, wash and pat dry. Cook the prawns over charcoal for about 5 minutes, turning once.

3. Add rice vermicelli to boiling water and boil for 2 minutes, drain and rinse under cold running water.

4. Heat oil in wok or frying pan, add green shallots and fry until softened. Arrange on warmed serving plates, top with prawns, then sprinkle with shallots and peanuts. Pour hot Nuoc Cham Sauce over top and sprinkle with chopped coriander.

Skewered Prawns

INGREDIENTS
500g/1 lb green prawns

Marinade
1 small onion, finely chopped
2 cloves garlic, crushed
1 teaspoon fresh ginger, chopped
55mL/2fl oz dry sherry
55mL/2fl oz olive oil
salt and freshly ground black pepper
12 bamboo skewers (soaked in water for 30 minutes)

METHOD
1. Wash prawns thoroughly. Do not remove shells.

2. Mix together ingredients to make marinade. Pour over prawns, and let stand for 1–2 hours in refrigerator.

3. Thread prawns on to skewers. Grill or barbecue for about 10 minutes (turning several times).

Serves 4

Barbecue Chilli Prawns

INGREDIENTS
1 kg/2 lb medium uncooked prawns, in their shells
225g/8oz chopped pawpaw
2 tablespoons chopped fresh mint
lime wedges
sliced chillies
Orange Marinade
2 tablespoons mild chilli powder
2 tablespoons chopped fresh oregano
2 cloves garlic, crushed
2 teaspoons grated orange rind
2 teaspoons grated lime rind
$^1/_4$ cup/55mL/2fl oz orange juice
$^1/_4$ cup/55mL/2fl oz lime juice

METHOD
1. To make marinade, place chilli powder, oregano, garlic, orange and lime rinds and orange and lime juices in a bowl and mix to combine. Add prawns, toss, cover and marinate in the refrigerator for 1 hour.

2. Drain prawns and cook on a preheated hot char-grill or barbecue plate (griddle) for 1 minute each side or until they change colour.

3. Place pawpaw and mint in bowl and toss to combine. To serve, pile prawns onto serving plates, top with pawpaw mixture and accompany with lime wedges and sliced chillies.

Serves 4

Barbecue Chilli Prawns

Prawn Satays

INGREDIENTS

**1kg/2 lb uncooked large prawns, shelled
and deveined, tails left intact**

Satay Sauce
2 teaspoons vegetable oil
1 onion, chopped
3 teaspoons ground cumin
255g/9oz crunchy peanut butter
1 cup/225mL/8fl oz chicken stock
3 tablespoons soy sauce

METHOD

1. Thread prawns onto eight skewers.

2. To make sauce, heat oil in a saucepan,
add onion and cumin and cook, stirring, for
3 minutes or until onion is soft.

3. Add peanut butter, stock and soy sauce
and cook over a medium heat, stirring, for
5 minutes or until sauce boils and thickens.

4. Brush prawns with sauce and cook on a
preheated barbecue grill for 2 minutes each side
or until prawns change colour and are cooked.
To serve, drizzle with any remaining sauce.

Makes 8

Scallop and Prawns en Brochette

INGREDIENTS

**500g/1lb green prawns, peeled,
deveived, tail intact**
400g/14oz scallops
225g/8oz pickling onions
6 bacon rashers
2 tablespoons olive oil
55g/2oz butter
2 tablespoons fresh dill, chopped
2 tablespoons parsely, chopped
2 spring onions, finely chopped
2 cloves garlic, crushed
freshly ground black pepper
2 tablespoons lemon juice
2 teaspoons grated lemon rind

METHOD

1. Parboil onions until almost tender, drain
and rinse under cold water. Remove rind
from bacon, cut each rasher into 3, roll each
section up.

2. Thread prawns, scallops and bacon onto
skewers, finish with an onion on the end of
each one.

3. Combine oil, butter, dill, parsley, spring
onions, garlic, pepper, lemon rind and juice,
add seafood skewers, stand at least 1 hour.

4. Remove from marinade, cook on
preheated barbecue grill until tender,
brushing occasionally with marinade.

Serves 6

3

Chilli Sesame Prawn Kebabs

INGREDIENTS

1 tablespoon vegetable oil

1 tablespoon Madras Curry paste

2 tablespoons finely grated fresh ginger

2 cloves garlic, crushed

2 tablespoons lime juice

$^{1}/_{2}$ cup/115g/4oz natural yohgurt

36 uncooked medium prawns, shelled and deveined, tails left intact

6 tablespoons sesame seeds, toasted

<u>Green Masala Onions</u>

30g/1oz ghee or butter

2 onions, cut into wedges

2 tablespoon Green Masala paste

METHOD

1. Place oil, curry paste, ginger, garlic, lime juice and yoghurt in a bowl and mix to combine. Add prawns and toss to coat. Cover and marinate in the refrigerator for 2-3 hours.

2. Drain prawns and thread 3 prawns onto an oiled skewer. Repeat with remaining prawns to make twelve kebabs. Toss kebabs in sesame seeds and cook on a lightly oiled, preheated medium barbecue or under a grill for 3 minutes each side or until prawns are cooked.

3. To make masala onions, melt ghee or butter in a saucepan over a medium heat, add onions and cook, stirring, for 5 minutes or until soft. Stir in masala paste and cook for 2 minutes longer or until heated through. Serve with prawns.

Serves 6

Chilli Sesame Prawn Kebabs

Honey and Chilli Prawns

INGREDIENTS

500g/1lb green king prawns
$^1/_4$ cup/55mL/2fl oz red wine
$^1/_2$ cup/115mL/4fl oz honey
$^1/_4$ teaspoon ground chilli
1 teaspoon mustard powder
soaked bamboo skewers

METHOD

1. Mix all ingredients except prawns together to make marinade.

2. Shell the prawns, leaving on the tails and de-vein. Place in a glass dish and add enough marinade to coat well. Cover and marinate in refrigerator for 1 hour. Thread the prawns onto skewers, either through the side or through the length.

3. Heat the barbecue to medium-high. Place a sheet of baking paper over the grill bars and place the prawns on the paper. Cook for 4-5 minutes each side: they will turn pink when cooked. Brush with marinade while cooking. Transfer to a platter. Remove skewers and serve immediately.

Serves 3-4

Teriyaki Prawns

INGREDIENTS

1kg/2lb fresh green prawns in shell
Teriyaki Marinade
$^1/_2$ cup/115mL/4fl oz soy sauce
2 tablespoons brown sugar
$^1/_2$ teaspoon ground ginger
2 tablespoons wine vinegar
1 clove garlic, crushed
2 tablespoons tomato sauce
bamboo skewers, soaked

METHOD

1. To make the marinade, mix all ingredients together and let stand for 1 hour for flavours to mix.

2. Shell the prawns, leaving the tails intact. Place in a non-metal dish and smother with the marinade. Cover and refrigerate for 1 or 2 hours. Thread onto soaked skewers.
(For small prawns thread 2 or 3 per skewer: for king prawns thread only one from tail-end to top).

3. Heat the barbecue and place a square of baking paper on the grill bars. Place the prawns on the grill, brushing with marinade on both sides as they cook. Cook until prawns turn pink in colour. Take care not to overcook.

Serves 4

Bacon and Prawns

INGREDIENTS

1 tablespoon Dijon mustard

1 clove garlic, crushed

$^1/_4$ red capsicum (pepper), finely chopped

1 tablespoon finely chopped fresh dill

2 tablespoons olive oil

2 tablespoons lemon juice

freshly ground black pepper

12 large cooked prawns, shelled with tails left intact

4 rashers lean bacon, cut into twelve 7$^1/_2$cm/3 in strips

METHOD

1. Place mustard, garlic, red capsicum (pepper), dill, oil, lemon juice and black pepper to taste in a bowl and mix to combine. Add prawns and toss to coat. Set aside to marinate for 30 minutes.

2. Preheat barbecue to a high heat. Drain prawns and reserve marinade. Wrap a strip of bacon around each prawn and thread onto bamboo skewers. Brush with reserved marinade and cook on lightly oiled barbecue, turning several times, for 2-3 minutes or until bacon is cooked and crisp.

Makes 4 kebabs

Avocado and Prawn Skewers

INGREDIENTS

2 avocados, cut into cubes

3 tablespoons lemon juice

20 cooked large prawns, shelled

10 cherry tomatoes, halved

10 bamboo skewers, lightly oiled

<u>Tomato Dipping Sauce</u>

$^1/_2$ cup/115g/4 oz sour cream

$^1/_2$ cup/115g/4 oz mayonnaise

2 tablespoons tomato sauce

2 teaspoons Worcestershire sauce

METHOD

1. Place avocado cubes in a bowl, pour lemon juice over and toss to coat. Thread 2 prawns, 2 avocado cubes and 2 tomato halves, alternately, onto bamboo skewers.

2. To make dipping sauce, place sour cream, mayonnaise, tomato sauce and Worcestershire sauce in a bowl and mix to combine. Serve sauce with kebabs for dipping.

Makes 10 kebabs

THE ORIENTAL
PRAWNS

Prawns and all other types of seafood are not only popular, but also extr
are fully utilised, and the seemingly endless variety of flavours produced

Beef with Prawns and Noodles

INGREDIENTS
155g/5¹/₂oz rice noodles
1 tablespoon peanut (groundnut) oil
2 cloves garlic, crushed
225g/8oz lean beef mince
225g/8oz uncooked prawns, shelled and
   deveined
2 tablespoons caster sugar
2 tablespoons white vinegar
1 tablespoon fish sauce
1 fresh red chilli, finely chopped
2 eggs, lightly beaten
115g/4oz bean sprouts
1 large carrot, grated
3 tablespoons chopped fresh coriander
   (cilantro)
2 tablespoons chopped blanched almonds

METHOD
1. Place noodles in a bowl, pour over boiling water to cover and set aside to stand for 8 minutes. Drain well.

2. Heat oil and garlic in a wok or large frying pan over a high heat, add beef and stir-fry for 2-3 minutes or until meat is brown. Add prawns and stir-fry for 1 minute. Stir in sugar, vinegar, fish sauce, and chilli and bring to boil, stirring constantly.

3. Add eggs to pan and cook, stirring, until set. Add bean sprouts, carrot and noodles and toss to combine. To serve, sprinkle with coriander (cilantro) and almonds.
Serves 4

Chilli Tempura

INGREDIENTS
vegetable oil for deep-frying
500g/1lb uncooked large prawns, peeled
   and deveined, tails left intact
12 snow peas (mangetout), trimmed
1 eggplant (aubergine), cut into thin slice
1 small head broccoli, broken into
   small florets
Tempura Batter
85g/3oz self-raising flour
¹/₂ cup/60g/2oz cornflour
1 teaspoon chilli powder
1 egg, lightly beaten
1 cup/225mL/8fl oz iced water
4 ice cubes

METHOD
1. To make batter, place flour, cornflour and chilli powder in a bowl, mix to combine and make a well in the centre. Whisk in egg and water and beat until smooth. Add ice cubes.

2. Heat oil in a deep saucepan until a cube o bread dropped in browns in 50 seconds.

3. Dip prawns, snow peas (mangetout), eggplant (aubergine) and broccoli florets in batter and deep-fry a few at a time for 3-4 minutes or until golden and crisp. Serve immediately.

Serving suggestion: All that is needed to make this a complete meal is a variety of purchased dipping sauces, chutneys,relishes and a tossed green salad.

4

...mportant to all Asian cultures. The vast array of bounties pulled out from the sea ...it little wonder why Oriental-style cuisine is so popular today.

Coconut Prawns

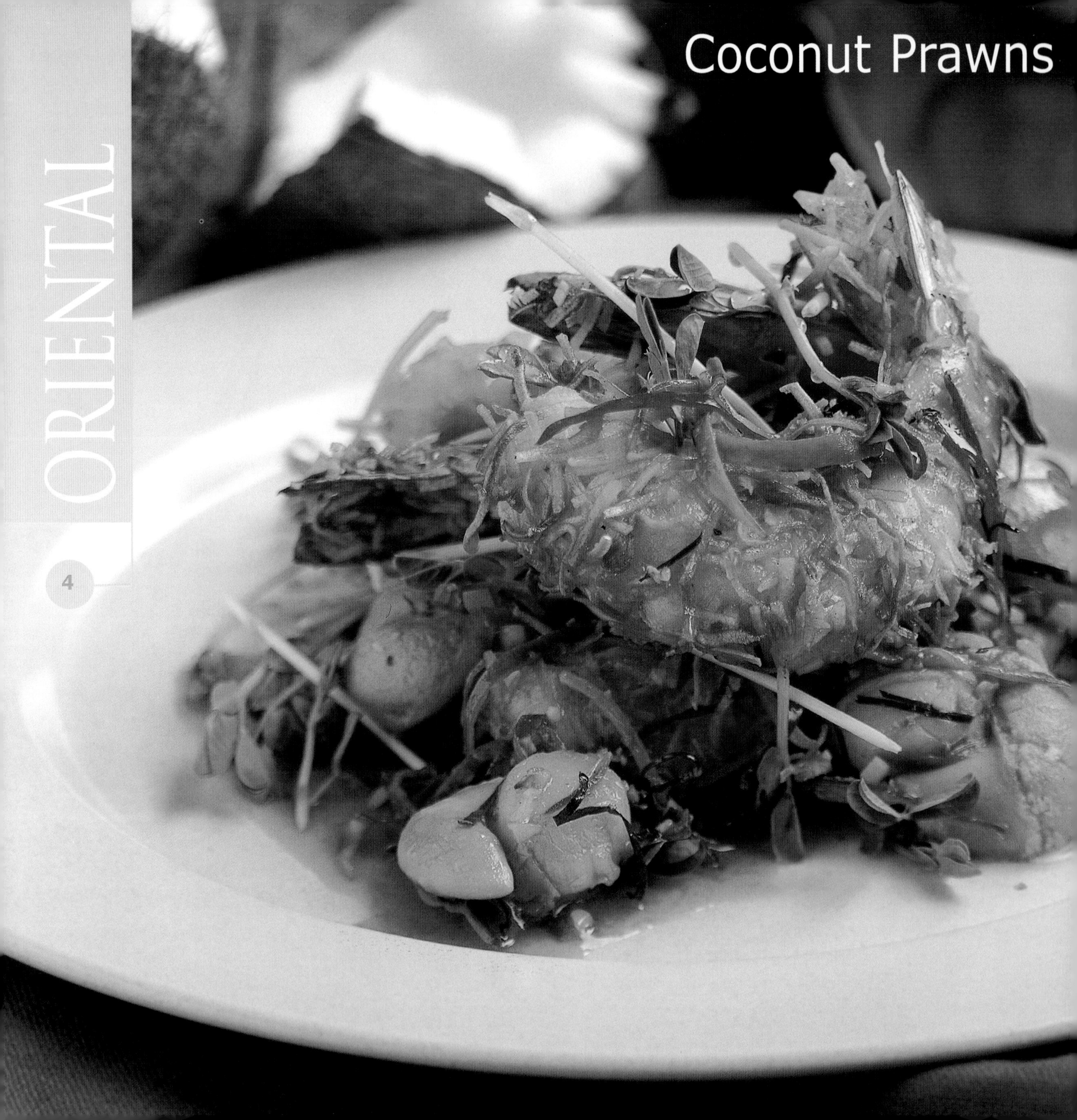

Scallops

Coconut Prawns and Scallops

INGREDIENTS

1kg/2 lb large uncooked prawns, shelled and deveined, tails left intact

3 egg whites, lightly beaten

85g/3oz shredded coconut

vegetable oil for deep-frying

1 tablespoon peanut oil

4 fresh red chillies, seeded and sliced

2 small fresh green chillies, seeded and sliced

2 cloves garlic, crushed

1 tablespoon shredded fresh ginger

3 kaffir lime leaves, finely shredded

375g/13^{1}/$_{4}$oz scallops

115g/4oz snow pea (mangetout) leaves or sprouts

2 tablespoons palm or brown sugar

^{1}/$_{4}$ cup/55mL/2fl oz lime juice

2 tablespoons Thai fish sauce (nam pla)

METHOD

1. Dip prawns in egg whites, then roll in coconut to coat. Heat vegetable oil in a large saucepan until a cube of bread dropped in browns in 50 seconds and cook prawns, a few at a time, for 2-3 minutes or until golden and crisp. Drain on absorbent kitchen paper and keep warm.

2. Heat peanut oil in a wok over a high heat, add red and green chillies, garlic, ginger and lime leaves and stir-fry for 2-3 minutes or until fragrant.

3. Add scallops to wok and stir-fry for 3 minutes or until opaque. Add cooked prawns, snow pea (mangetout) leaves or sprouts, sugar, lime juice and fish sauce and stir-fry for 2 minutes or until heated.

Serves 6

Sour Prawns Curry

INGREDIENTS

500mL/17¹/₂fl oz coconut milk

1 teaspoon shrimp paste

2 tablespoons Thai Green Curry Paste

1 stalk fresh lemon grass, finely chopped or

¹/₂ teaspoon dried lemon grass, soaked in
  hot water until soft

2 fresh green chillies, chopped

1 tablespoon ground cumin

1 tablespoon ground coriander

500g/1lb uncooked large prawns, shelled
  and deveined

3 cucumbers, halved and sliced

115g/4oz canned bamboo shoots, drained

1 tablespoon tamarind concentrate,
  dissolved in 3 tablespoons hot water

METHOD

1. Place coconut milk, shrimp paste, curry
paste, lemon grass, chillies, cumin and coriander
in a wok and bring to simmering over a medium
heat. Simmer, stirring occasionally, for 10
minutes.

2. Stir prawns, cucumbers, bamboo shoots and
tamarind mixture into coconut milk mixture and
cook, stirring occasionally, for 10 minutes or
until prawns are cooked.

Serves 4

Stir-Fry Chilli Prawns

INGREDIENTS
1 teaspoon vegetable oil
1 teaspoon sesame oil
3 cloves garlic, crushed
3 fresh red chillies, chopped
1kg/2.2 lb uncooked medium
  prawns, shelled and deveined
1 tablespoon brown sugar
1/3 cup/85mL/3fl oz tomato
  juice
1 tablespoon soy sauce

METHOD
1. Heat vegetable and sesame oils
together in a wok over a medium
heat, add garlic and chillies and
stir-fry for 1 minute. Add prawns and
stir-fry for 2 minutes or until they
change colour.

2. Stir in sugar, tomato juice and
soy sauce and stir-fry, for 3 minutes
or until sauce is heated through.

Serves 4

FOR A COMPLETE MEAL, SERVE PRAWNS WITH
BOILED RICE OR NOODLES OF YOUR
CHOICE AND STIR-FRIED VEGETABLES.

Spring Roll Baskets

INGREDIENTS

vegetable oil for deep-frying

**8 spring roll or wonton wrappers, each
  12$^1/_2$ cm/5 in square**

**2 tablespoons unsalted cashews, toasted
  and chopped**

<u>**Pork and Prawn Filling**</u>

1 tablespoon peanut (groundnut) oil

2 teaspoons finely grated fresh ginger

1 small fresh red chilli, finely chopped

4 spring onions, finely chopped

220g/8oz lean pork mince

**125g/4oz uncooked prawns, shelled and
  deveined**

1 tablespoon soy sauce

2 teaspoons fish sauce

2 teaspoons honey

2 teaspoons lemon juice

30g/1oz bean sprouts

1 small carrot, cut into thin strips

1 tablespoon finely chopped fresh coriander

METHOD

1. Heat vegetable oil in a large saucepan until a cube of bread dropped in browns in 50 seconds. Place 2 spring roll or wonton wrappers, diagonally, one on top of the other, so that the corners are not matching. Shape wrappers around the base of a small ladle, lower into hot oil and cook for 3-4 minutes. During cooking keep wrappers submerged in oil by pushing down with the ladle to form a basket shape. Drain on absorbent kitchen paper. Repeat with remaining wrappers to make four baskets.

2. To make filling, heat peanut (groundnut) oil in a frying pan, add ginger, chilli and spring onions and stir-fry for 1 minute. Add pork and stir-fry for 5 minutes or until meat is brown. Add prawns, soy sauce, fish sauce, honey, lemon juice, bean sprouts, carrot and coriander and stir-fry for 4-5 minutes longer or until prawns change colour.

3. To serve, spoon filling into baskets and sprinkle with cashews.

Serves 4

4

Thai Garlic Prawns

Thai Garlic Prawns

INGREDIENTS

6 cloves garlic, crushed

6 tablespoons chopped fresh coriander

3 tablespoons vegetable oil

500g/1lb uncooked large prawns, shelled
and deveined, tails left intact

$^3/_4$ cup/185mL/6$^1/_2$fl oz water

$^1/_4$ cup/55mL/2fl oz fish sauce

1 tablespoon sugar

freshly ground black pepper

METHOD

1. Place garlic, coriander and
2 tablespoons oil in a food processor or
blender and process until smooth.

2. Heat remaining oil in a large wok or
frying pan, add garlic mixture and stir-fry
for 2 minutes. Add prawns and stir-fry to
coat with garlic mixture. Stir in water, fish
sauce, sugar and black pepper to taste
and stir-fry until prawns are cooked.
Serves 4

Gingered King Prawns

INGREDIENTS

5cm/2in green ginger

3 large green shallots

$^1/_2$ cup/115mL/4fl oz peanut oil

$^1/_2$ teaspoon crushed dried chilli

black pepper to taste

1 tablespoon soy sauce

1kg/2.2lb large green king prawns

METHOD

1. Peel the ginger and cut half of it into
thin slices. Cut the other half into julienne
strips. Cut the green shallots (half tops as
well) into 5cm/2in lengths. Heat oil, add
ginger slices, shallot and chilli. Remove
from heat, add black pepper and soy
sauce and allow to infuse until completely
cool.

2. Wash, then dry prawns and with small
scissors, cut along top of shell and
remove dark vein down the back. Leave
shell and tail on and remove heads if you
prefer. Toss the prawns in the cooled oil
mixture and leave to marinate for several
hours.

3. When ready to serve, heat grill until
very hot and arrange the prawns on the
grilling rack. Sprinkle with oil marinade
and half ginger strips and cook until pink,
then turn and repeat on other side.
Serves 4

Prawn Toasts

INGREDIENTS

500g/1lb peeled cooked prawns, deveined
6 spring onions, chopped
2 teaspoon grated fresh root ginger
2 teaspoon light soy sauce
1/2 teaspoon sesame oil
2 egg whites
6 slices white bread
30g/1oz fresh white breadcrumbs
oil for deep frying

METHOD

1. Combine prawns, spring onions, ginger, soy sauce and sesame oil in a blender or food processor. Blend until roughly chopped. Add egg whites and blend until combined.

2. Remove crusts from bread slices, spread them with prawn mixture, then cut each slice into three strips.

3. Dip prawn-coated side of each bread strip into breadcrumbs. Deep fry bread strips in hot oil until light golden brown. Drain on paper towels and serve at once, with a coriander garnish, if liked.

Makes 18

Prawns with Coriander Butter

INGREDIENTS

750g/1^1/2lb large king prawns, shelled, deveined, tail intact
1/4 cup/55mL/2fl oz olive oil
1 bunch coriander (cilantro)
2 cloves garlic, crushed
salt, to taste
2 tablespoons lemon juice
1/4 cup/55mL/2fl oz each of dry white wine and dry vermouth
1 tablespoon white wine vinegar
2 tablespoons spring onions, chopped
85g/3oz butter
225g/8oz snow peas
1/2 red capsicum (pepper), cut into thin strips
115g/4oz oriental or button mushrooms

METHOD

1. Marinate prawns for a few hours in the oil, half the coriander (cilantro) sprigs, garlic, salt and lemon juice.

2. Make the sauce by adding the wine, vermouth, vinegar and spring onions. Bring to the boil and reduce to about 3 tablespoons. Over a little heat whisk in butter in small pieces until the sauce thickens. Season with a little lemon juice, salt and pepper. Chop remaining coriander (cilantro) and stir into Butter Sauce.

3. Heat a large frying pan and sauté the prawns for about 2 minutes. At the same time have a pan of boiling salted water ready and drop in the snow peas, red capsicum (pepper) and mushrooms for a minute.

4. Drain and toss the vegetables with the prawns in the frying pan. Divide the prawns on 4 plates, reheat the sauce and spoon over each serving.

Serves 4

Stir-Fried Tamarind Prawns

INGREDIENTS

2 tablespoons tamarind pulp
125mL/4¹/₂fl oz water
2 teaspoons vegetable oil
3 stalks fresh lemon grass, chopped or
2 teaspoons finely grated lemon rind
2 fresh red chillies, chopped
500g/1 lb medium uncooked prawns,
  shelled and deveined, tails intact
2 green (unripe) mangoes, peeled and
  thinly sliced
3 tablespoons chopped fresh coriander
  (cilantro) leaves
2 tablespoons brown sugar
2 tablespoons lime juice

METHOD

1. Place tamarind pulp and water in a bowl and stand for 20 minutes. Strain, reserve liquid and set aside. Discard solids.

2. Heat oil in a wok or frying pan over a high heat, add lemon grass or rind and chillies and stir-fry for 1 minute. Add prawns and stir-fry for 2 minutes or until they change colour.

3. Add mangoes, coriander, sugar, lime juice and tamarind liquid and stir-fry for 5 minutes or until prawns are cooked.

Serves 4

Sesame Prawn Cakes

INGREDIENTS

315g/11oz uncooked, shelled and deveined
  prawns
250g/8³/₄oz fresh crab meat
3 spring onions, chopped
2 tablespoons finely chopped fresh basil
1 fresh red chilli, finely chopped
1 teaspoon ground cumin
1 teaspoon paprika
1 egg white
140g/5oz sesame seeds
1 tablespoon vegetable oil

METHOD

1. Preheat barbecue to a medium heat. Place prawns, crab meat, spring onions, basil, chilli, cumin, paprika and egg white into a food processor and process until well combined.

2. Take 4 tablespoons of mixture, shape into a pattie and roll in sesame seeds to coat. Repeat with remaining mixture to make six patties.

3. Heat oil on barbecue plate (griddle) for 2-3 minutes or until hot, add patties and cook for 10 minutes each side or until patties are golden and cooked.

Serves 6

4

Lemon Grass Prawns

INGREDIENTS

1kg/2 lb uncooked medium prawns
3 stalks fresh lemon grass, finely chopped
2 spring onions, chopped
2 small fresh red chillies, finely chopped
2 cloves garlic, crushed
2 tablespoons finely grated fresh ginger
1 teaspoon shrimp paste
1 tablespoon brown sugar
125mL/4^{1}/$_{2}$fl oz coconut milk

METHOD

1. Wash prawns, leaving shells and heads intact, and place in a shallow glass or ceramic dish.

2. Place lemon grass, spring onions, chillies, garlic, ginger and shrimp paste in a food processor or blender and process until smooth. Add sugar and coconut milk and process to combine. Spoon mixture over prawns, toss to combine, cover and marinate in the refrigerator for 3-4 hours.

3. Preheat barbecue to a high heat. Drain prawns, place on barbecue and cook, turning several times, for 5 minutes or until prawns change colour.
Serve immediately.

Serves 4

Fresh lemon grass and shrimp paste are available from Oriental food shops and some supermarkets. Lemon grass can also be purchased dried; if using dried lemon grass, soak in hot water for 20 minutes or until soft before using. It is also available in bottles from supermarkets. Use this in the same way as you would fresh lemon grass.

Pad Thai

INGREDIENTS

315g/10oz fresh or dried rice noodles

2 teaspoons vegetable oil

4 red or golden shallots, chopped

3 fresh red chillies, chopped

2 tablespoons shredded fresh ginger

225g/8oz boneless chicken breast fillets,
  chopped

225g/8oz medium uncooked prawns,
  shelled and deveined

55g/2oz roasted peanuts, chopped

1 tablespoon sugar

4 tablespoons lime juice

3 tablespoons fish sauce

2 tablespoons light soy sauce

125g/4^1/2oz tofu, chopped

55g/2oz bean sprouts

4 tablespoons fresh coriander (cilantro)
  leaves

3 tablespoons fresh mint leaves

lime wedges to serve

METHOD

1. Place noodles in a bowl and pour over boiling water to cover. If using fresh noodles soak for 2 minutes; if using dried noodles soak for 5-6 minutes or until soft. Drain well and set aside.

2. Heat oil in a frying pan or wok over a high heat, add shallots, chillies and ginger and stir-fry for 1 minute. Add chicken and prawns and stir-fry for 4 minutes or until cooked.

3. Add noodles, peanuts, sugar, lime juice and fish and soy sauces and stir-fry for 4 minutes or until heated through. Stir in tofu, bean sprouts, coriander (cilantro) and mint and cook for 1-2 minutes or until heated through. Serve with lime wedges.

Serves 4

Braised Prawns with Chinese Greens

INGREDIENTS

750g/1^1/2 lb green prawns, shelled and
deveined
1 tablespoon Chinese wine or dry sherry
1 teaspoon cornflour
1 teaspoon soy sauce
12 snow peas (mangetout)
1 punnet snow peas or Chinese flowering
cabbage
5 tablespoons oil
<u>**Seasoning**</u>
^{1}/2 teaspoon salt
^{1}/2 teaspoon sugar
2 teaspoon soy sauce
1 teaspoon sesame oil

METHOD

1. Put prawns into bowl with wine, cornflour and soy sauce. Mix well, cover and chill for at least 30 minutes.

2. Heat 4 tablespoons oil in a wok and cook prawns until colour changes. Remove. Add rest of oil to wok and cook vegetables for 2 minutes.

3. Return prawns to wok and add seasonings. Toss until heated through and serve immediately.

Serves 4

Deep-fried Chilli Coconut Prawns

INGREDIENTS
3 eggs, lightly beaten
$^1/_2$ teaspoon chilli powder
125g/4$^1/_2$oz breadcrumbs, made from
 stale bread
125g/4$^1/_2$oz shredded coconut
24 green prawns, shelled, deveined, tail intact
125g/4$^1/_2$oz flour
vegetable oil for deep-frying

METHOD
1. Combine eggs and chilli powder in a shallow dish. Combine breadcrumbs and coconut in a separate shallow dish.

2. Roll prawns in flour to coat thickly. Dip in egg mixture. Roll in breadcrumb mixture to coat.

3. Heat oil in a saucepan until a cube of bread dropped in browns in 50 seconds. Deep-fry prawns, in batches, for 2 minutes or until golden and crisp. Drain on absorbent kitchen paper.

Serves 4

Singapore Noodles

INGREDIENTS

500g/1lb fresh egg noodles
2 teaspoons vegetable oil
2 eggs, lightly beaten
1 teaspoon sesame oil
1 onion, chopped
1 red capsicum (pepper), chopped
2 cloves garlic, crushed
1 fresh red chilli, chopped
8 uncooked large prawns, shelled and deveined
250g/8^1/2oz Chinese barbecued pork or Chinese roast pork, thinly sliced
6 spring onions, sliced
2 tablespoons fresh coriander leaves
1 teaspoon sugar
1 teaspoon ground turmeric
^{1}/2 teaspoon ground cumin
2 tablespoons soy sauce

METHOD

1. Place noodles in a bowl of boiling water and stand for 5 minutes. Drain and set aside.

2. Heat vegetable oil in a wok over a medium heat, add eggs and swirl wok to coat base and sides. Cook for 2 minutes or until set. Remove omelette from wok, cool, then roll up and cut into thin strips.

3. Heat sesame oil in a clean wok over a high heat, add onion, red pepper, garlic and chilli and stir-fry for 3 minutes. Add prawns and pork and stir-fry for 3 minutes longer.

4. Add noodles, egg strips, spring onions, coriander, sugar, turmeric, cumin and soy sauce to wok and stir-fry for 3 minutes or until heated through.

Serves 4

Singapor

Noodles

Tiger Prawns with Oriental Dipping Sauce

INGREDIENTS

10 green tiger prawns, shelled, deveined, tails intact

1 tablespoon sunflower oil

4 cos lettuce leaves

fresh coriander (cilantro) to garnish

<u>Dipping Sauce</u>

1 clove garlic, crushed

$1/2$ teaspoon sugar

few drops of Tabasco

finely grated rind and juice of $1/2$ lime

3 tablespoons sunflower oil

salt and ground black pepper

METHOD

1. To make the dipping sauce, mix together all ingredients, season accordingly.

2. Heat oil in a frying pan, then fry prawns for 3-4 minutes or until pink and cooked through.

3. Arrange lettuce leaves on serving plates, scatter over prawns and garnish with coriander (cilantro). Serve with dipping sauce.

Serves 2

Tiger Prawns, Snowpeas and Mango Stir Fry

INGREDIENTS

400g/14oz green tiger prawns, shelled, deveined, tails intact

2 tablespoons vegetable oil

$1^1/2$ tablespoons grated fresh ginger

300g/10^1/2oz snowpeas (mangetout)

bunch spring onions, sliced

1 large mango, peeled and thinly sliced

2 tablespoons light soy sauce

METHOD

1. Heat the oil in a wok, add ginger and prawns and stir-fry for 2 minutes or until the prawns are just turning pink.

2. Add the snowpeas (mangetout) and spring onions and stir-fry for a further minute to soften slightly. Stir in the mango and soy sauce and stir-fry for 1 minute to heat through.

South-east Asian Pan-fried Prawns

INGREDIENTS

500g/1 lb green prawns, shelled, deveined, tail intact

3 small red chillies, deseeded and chopped

2 cloves garlic, chopped

$2^1/2$cm/1 in piece fresh root ginger, chopped

1 eshallot, chopped

2 tablespoons vegetable oil

1 onion, chopped

2 tomatoes, quartered

1 teaspoon sugar

salt

METHOD

1. Blend the chillies, garlic, ginger and shallot to a paste in a food processor or with a pestle and mortar. Heat the oil in a large, heavy-based frying pan or wok over a high heat, then fry the onion for 2 minutes to soften slightly. Add the paste and stir-fry for 1 minute to release the flavour.

2. Add the prawns and tomatoes, mixing thoroughly, then sprinkle over the sugar and salt to taste. Fry for 3-5 minutes, until the prawns turn pink and are cooked through, stirring often.

Serves 4

Fried Rice with Prawns

INGREDIENTS

150g/$5^1/4$oz long-grain rice

salt

75g/$2^1/2$ oz frozen peas

2 tablespoon vegetable oil

3 cloves garlic, peeled and chopped roughly

2 spring onions, thinly sliced

1 egg, beaten

100g/$3^1/2$ oz cooked, peeled school prawns

METHOD

1. Rinse the rice in a sieve. Bring a large saucepan of water to the boil, then add the rice and $1/2$ teaspoon of salt. Simmer for 10 minutes or until the rice is tender, then drain thoroughly. Meanwhile, bring a small pan of water to the boil, add the peas and cook for 3-4 minutes, until softened.

2. Heat a wok or a large heavy-based frying pan over a medium heat. Add the oil and rotate the wok or pan for 1 minute to coat the base and lower sides.

3. Add the garlic and spring onions and fry, stirring constantly with a wooden spoon, for 30 seconds. Then add the beaten egg and stir briskly for 30 seconds or until it scrambles.

4. Add the cooked rice, peas and prawns and stir over the heat for 3 minutes or until everything is heated through and mixed in with the egg and spring onions. Season with a pinch of salt.

Butterflied Prawns

INGREDIENTS

500g/1 lb green king prawns
1 ham steak
1 zucchini (courgette)
6 shallots
2 tablespoons vegetable oil

Dipping Sauce
2 tablespoons cornflour, blended with
55mL/2fl oz water
1 cup/225mL/8fl oz water
1 chicken stock cube
2 tablespoons sherry
2 tablespoons soy sauce
2 tablespoons ginger
1 clove garlic, crushed

METHOD

1. Shell and devein prawns, leaving tails intact. Make a shallow cut along back of prawn. Cut a 1cm/^{1}/$_2$in slit right through the centre of each prawn.

2. Cut ham, zucchini (courgette) and shallots into thin straws, 5cm/2in long. Push a piece of each through the slit in the prawn.

3. Heat vegetable oil in wok or frying pan, add prawns and stir fry for 1 minute.

4. Stir in blended cornflour, water, stock cube, sherry, soy sauce, ginger and garlic, stir over heat until mixture boils and thickens; use as a dipping sauce for prawns.

Makes 24

Vietnamese Crêpes with a Dipping Sauce

INGREDIENTS

For Crêpes

250g/8¹/₂oz rice flour

1 teaspoon salt

1¹/₂ teaspoons sugar

1 cup/225mL/8fl oz coconut milk (tinned)

1 cup/225mL/8fl oz water

¹/₂ teaspoon ground turmeric

200g/7oz shelled king prawns

200g/7oz bean shoots

100g/3¹/₂ oz pork fillet or chicken

1 onion, sliced

peanut oil (for frying)

For Dressing

3 teaspoons fish sauce

5 teaspoons sugar

2 tablespoons water

1 tiny red chilli (minced)

1 clove garlic (minced)

Vietnamese mint leaves (for serving)

iceberg lettuce leaves (for serving)

METHOD

1. First, make the batter. Mix together the rice flour, salt, sugar, coconut milk, water and turmeric until the batter is smooth.

2. Wash and dry the prawns and chop roughly. Wash the bean shoots and set aside.

3. Dice the pork or chicken.

4. Heat a large frying pan and pour in a little oil. Add the pork, onion and prawns, and cook, stirring constantly until the prawns change colour and the pork is cooked through.

5. Pour enough batter over the mixture to cover the ingredients, top with some bean shoots and cover with a lid. Cook for 2 minutes until crisp. Turn over and cook the other side until golden.

6. Make the dressing by mixing all the ingredients together, stirring well.

To serve, place a Vietnamese mint leaf on a piece of the crêpe. Enclose in a lettuce leaf and drizzle some dressing over. Eat immediately.

Variation: To make a vegetarian crêpe, replace the pork and prawns with 1 medium carrot and half a medium-sized red capsicum (both julienned finely) and proceed as above.

Vietnames

rêpes with a
Dipping Sauce

Tuna and Prawn Sushi

INGREDIENTS

12 large cooked prawns, shelled, deveined, tails left intact

2 teaspoons wasabi powder

125g/4 oz sashimi (fresh) tuna

1 sheet nori (seaweed), cut into strips (optional)

soy sauce

Sushi Rice

500g/1 lb short grain rice

600mL/21fl oz water

2 tablespoons sweet sake or sherry

4 tablespoons rice vinegar

2 tablespoons sugar

$1/2$ teaspoon salt

METHOD

1. For the rice, wash rice several times in cold water and set aside to drain for 30 minutes. Place rice and water in a large saucepan and bring to the boil, cover and cook, without stirring, over a low heat for 15 minutes. Remove pan from heat and set aside for 10 minutes.

2. Place sake or sherry, vinegar, sugar and salt in a small saucepan and bring to the boil. Remove pan from heat and set aside to cool.

3. Turn rice out into a large shallow dish, pour over vinegar mixture and toss gently until rice has cooled to room temperature. Take a tablespoon of rice in your hand and gently squeeze it to form a neat oval. Place on a serving platter and repeat with remaining rice to make 24 ovals.

4. Split prawns on the underside – taking care not to cut all the way through – and flatten them out. Mix wasabi powder with a few drops of water to make a smooth paste and dab a little on each rice oval. Top twelve rice ovals with prawns.

5. Cut tuna into twelve 2 x 4 cm/$3/4$ x $1^{1}/2$ in strips each 5 mm/$1/5$ in thick. Top remaining rice ovals with tuna strips. Wrap a strip of nori (seaweed), if using, around each sushi. Serve sushi with soy sauce for dipping.

Makes 24

4

Sesame Coconut King Prawns with Mango Salsa

INGREDIENTS

12 raw king prawns, peeled tail left on
salt and pepper to taste
flour for dusting
1 egg, beaten
1 cup/125g/4^1/2oz sesame seeds
1 cup/90g/3oz coconut threads
1 mango, peeled and finely diced
^{1}/2 small Spanish onion, finely diced
2 tablespoons coriander (cilantro), chopped
juice of 1 lime
2 tablespoons butter or olive oil
assorted greens of your choice

METHOD

1. Butterfly the prawns then dust with salt, pepper and flour. Dip in egg, allowing the excess to run off, then dredge in a mixture of sesame seeds and coconut. Set aside.

2. Mix the mango, onion coriander (cilantro) and lime juice in a bowl and season to taste.

3. Heat the butter or olive oil in a frypan, add the king prawns and fry over a high heat for 1-2 minutes each side until golden.

4. To serve, arrange some leaves on each plate and top with 3 cooked prawns and generous spoonful of mango salsa.

Honeyed Prawns Chow Mein

INGREDIENTS

2 tablespoons vegetable oil
1 clove garlic, crushed
1 onion, petalled
2 stalks celery, sliced
125g/4^1/2oz button mushrooms, sliced
55g/2oz snow peas (mangetout)
125g/4^1/2oz canned bamboo shoots, drained
125g/4^1/2oz canned water chestnuts, drained and sliced
750g/1^1/2 lb large uncooked prawns, shelled and deveined, with tails intact
^{1}/4cup/75g/2^1/2oz honey
1 tablespoon dry sherry
1 tablespoon soy sauce
1 tablespoon sesame seeds, toasted

METHOD

1. Heat oil in a wok or frying pan over a medium heat, add garlic and stir-fry for 30 seconds. Add onion and celery and stir-fry for 1 minute. Add mushrooms, snow peas (mangetout), bamboo shoots and water chestnuts and stir-fry for 3 minutes longer or until vegetables are just tender.

2. Add prawns and stir-fry for 2 minutes or until prawns just change colour. Add honey, sherry and soy sauce and stir-fry for 2 minutes longer or until mixture is heated through. Sprinkle with sesame seeds and serve immediately.

Sesame Coconut King Prawns with Mango Salsa

4

Steamed Prawns with Ginger and Soy Sauce

INGREDIENTS

1 bunch fresh coriander (cilantro)
5cm/2 in piece fresh ginger
2 tablespoons each sesame and vegetable oil
2 tablespoons finely sliced green spring onions
light soy sauce
1kg/2lb small-medium green prawns

METHOD

1. Wash coriander (cilantro) and cut roots and stems off, chopping roughly. Reserve the leaves. Pour water into a pan to a depth of about 2^1/2cm/1 in and add the chopped coriander (cilantro) stems.

2. To make sauce, peel and shred the green ginger into very fine slivers. Heat oils almost to smoking point, remove from heat and add ginger and spring onions. Leave to cool 15 minutes and stir in soy sauce.

3. Line one large or several small steamer baskets with coriander (cilantro) leaves and place the prawns in one layer on top. Season with a little salt and cover with more coriander (cilantro) leaves. Steam with the lid on over the coriander water for 5 minutes or until prawns have all turned pink.

4. Remove from heat and transfer to a serving platter. Serve with the ginger and soy sauce.

Serves 4

Nasi Goreng

INGREDIENTS

55mL/2fl oz vegetable oil
1 onion, sliced
3 spring onions, chopped
250g/8¹/₂oz diced pork
125g/4¹/₂oz shelled uncooked prawns
(optional)
4 cups/750g/1¹/₂ lb cooked rice or
2 cups/440g/14oz raw rice, cooked
1 red capsicum (pepper), chopped
45g/1¹/₂ oz sultanas or raisins
45g/1¹/₂ oz cashews or peanuts (optional)
1 teaspoon chopped fresh red chilli
2 tablespoons soy sauce

CHINESE OMELETTE
2 eggs
2 teaspoons water
freshly ground black pepper

METHOD

1. To make omelette, place eggs, water and black pepper to taste in a bowl and whisk to combine. Heat a lightly greased wok or frying pan over a medium heat, add half the egg mixture and tilt pan to thinly coat base. Cook for 1-2 minutes or until underside of omelette is set, flip omelette and cook for 10 seconds. Remove and set aside to cool. Use remaining egg mixture to make a second omelette. Stack omelettes, roll up and cut into fine shreds. Set aside.

2. Heat half the oil in a wok or large frying pan over a medium heat, add onion and spring onions and stir-fry for 3-4 minutes or until onion is tender. Add pork and stir-fry for 2-3 minutes. Add prawns, if using, and stir-fry for 1-2 minutes longer or until prawns change colour. Remove mixture from pan and set aside.

3. Heat remaining oil in same pan, add rice, red pepper, sultanas or raisins, cashews or peanuts, if using, chilli and soy sauce and stir-fry for 2 minutes. Return pork mixture to pan and stir-fry for 1 minute or until heated through. Top with omelette strips and serve immediately.

Serves 4

MEDITTERANEAN
PRAWNS

The lands lapping the Mediterranean, among them Fran‹ of them a culinary style that is wholly unique. The Spanish h Greeks are synonymous with their uses of herbs,

Prawns with Sauce Verte

INGREDIENTS

750g/1¹/₂lb uncooked prawns, shelled
  and deveined, leaving tail shells intact
170mL/6fl oz dry vermouth
2-6 spring onions, chopped
1 sprig fresh parsley
1 bay leaf
salt
freshly ground black pepper
Sauce Verte
3-4 spinach or young silverbeet leaves,
  stems removed
170g/6oz mayonnaise
3-4 tablespoon finely chopped fresh parsley
2 tablespoon snipped fresh chives

1 tablespoon finely chopped fresh dill or
¹/₂ teaspoon dried
For Garnish
8 small leaves mixed lettuce
chopped fresh parsley and slivered spring
onion greens or chives

METHOD

1. Place vermouth, spring onions, parsley sprig and bay leaf in a saucepan, season to taste with salt and black pepper and bring to simmering. Add prawns and simmer gently for 2-3 minutes or until tender and pink. Drain and cool.

2. To make sauce, steam spinach or silverbeet in a saucepan, covered, over moderate heat for 1 minute only. Cool quickly in cold water, drain and pat dry on paper towels. Finely chop. Place mayonnaise in a bowl, add spinach, parsley, chives and dill and mix to combine.

3. To serve, smear a little sauce in a semi-circle on four entrée plates. Arrange prawns on sauce, garnish with lettuce leaves and sprinkle with parsley and spring onions or chives.

Serves 4

Prawns in Tomato Sauce

INGREDIENTS

55g/2oz butter
1 large onion (finely chopped)
1 clove garlic, crushed
4 large ripe tomatoes, skinned and chopped
1 tablespoon tomato paste
2 cups/450mL/16fl oz dry white wine
1 bay leaf
salt and pepper
1kg/2 lb cooked prawns
6 shallots (chopped)

METHOD

1. Heat butter in pan, add onion and garlic. Cook until onion is soft.

2. Add tomatoes, tomato paste, wine and bayleaf, and season (to taste) with salt and pepper. Bring to boil, reduce heat, and simmer (uncovered) for 30 minutes or until sauce is reduced and thickened. Remove bay leaf.

3. Add shelled prawns and chopped shallots, and simmer gently until prawns are heated through.

Serves 4

ly, Greece and Spain, all have special attributes that give each
ella, France has bouillabaisse, Italians are famous for their pastas and the
and cheeses. Enjoy our selection of inspiring prawn dishes!

Chilli Prawn Pizza

INGREDIENTS

1 frozen pizza base
3 tablespoons tomato paste (purée)
2 teaspoons vegetable oil
1 teaspoon ground cumin
3 fresh red chillies, seeded and chopped
2 cloves garlic, crushed
2 tablespoons lemon juice
500g/1lb uncooked prawns,
  shelled and deveined
1 red capsicum (pepper), sliced
1 yellow or green capsicum (pepper), sliced
2 tablespoons chopped fresh coriander
  (cilantro)
2 tablespoons grated Parmesan cheese
freshly ground black pepper

METHOD

1. Place pizza base on a lightly greased
baking tray, spread with tomato paste (purée)
and set aside.

2. Heat oil in a frying pan over a medium
heat, add cumin, chillies and garlic and cook,
stirring, for 1 minute.

3. Stir in lemon juice and prawns and cook
for 3 minutes longer or until prawns just
change colour and are almost cooked.

4. Top pizza base with red capsicum
(pepper), yellow or green capsicum (pepper),
then with prawn mixture, coriander, parmesan
cheese and black pepper to taste. Bake for 20
minutes or until base is crisp and golden.

Serves 4

Leek and Prawn Risotto

Penne with Saffron and Prawns

INGREDIENTS

500g/1lb penne
500g/1lb cooked prawns, shelled
 and deveined
125g/4oz snow peas (mangetout),
 blanched
<u>Saffron Sauce</u>
30g/1oz butter
1 tablespoon flour
1 cup/225mL/8fl oz reduced-fat milk
$^1/_2$ teaspoon saffron threads or pinch
 saffron powder
1 tablespoon chopped fresh sage
 or $^1/_2$ teaspoon dried sage

METHOD

1. Cook pasta in boiling water in a large saucepan following packet directions. Drain, set aside and keep warm.

2. To make sauce, melt butter in a small saucepan over a medium heat, stir in flour and cook for 1 minute. Remove pan from heat and whisk in milk, saffron and sage. Return pan to heat and cook, stirring, for 3-4 minutes or until sauce boils and thickens.

3. Add prawns and snow peas (mangetout) to hot pasta and toss to combine. Top with sauce and serve immediately.

Serves 4

INGREDIENTS

15g/$^1/_2$ oz butter
4 leeks, sliced
500g/1 lb medium uncooked prawns, shelled
 and deveined
500g/1lb arborio or risotto rice
1 litre/1$^3/_4$ pt hot fish or vegetable stock
1 cup/225mL/8fl oz dry white wine
1 tablespoon canned green peppercorns,
 drained

METHOD

1. Melt butter in a saucepan over a low heat, add leeks and cook, stirring occasionally, for 8 minutes or until leeks are soft, golden and caramelised. Add prawns and cook, stirring, for 3 minutes or until they just change colour. Remove prawn mixture from pan and set aside.

2. Add rice to pan and cook over a medium heat, stirring, for 4 minutes. Stir in 185mL/6$^1/_2$fl oz hot stock and 55mL/2fl oz wine and cook, stirring constantly, over a medium heat until liquid is absorbed. Continue adding stock and wine as described, stirring constantly and allowing stock to be absorbed before adding any more.

3. Return prawn mixture to pan, add green peppercorns. Mix gently to combine and cook for 3 minutes longer or until heated through.

Serves 4

Penne with Saffron and Prawns

Spanish Carrot and Prawn Salad

INGREDIENTS

700g/1¹/2 lbs carrots
4 cloves garlic
1 tablespoon fresh rosemary
55mL/2fl oz virgin olive oil
1 teaspoon ground cumin
2 teaspoons mild paprika
45mL/1¹/2 fl oz white wine vinegar
salt and freshly ground pepper to taste
500g/1 lb large peeled, cooked prawns
   (tail on)
¹/4 bunch parsley, chopped

METHOD

1. Peel and trim the carrots, then slice on the diagonal into 5mm/¹/4 in slices. Add the carrots to some salted boiling water and cook for 3-4 minutes or until almost crisp-tender, then drain.

2. Peel garlic and pound in a mortar and pestle with the fresh rosemary until ground.

3. Heat a teaspoon of oil in a small frypan and add the garlic and rosemary mixture, cumin and paprika and sauté for a minute or two. Remove from the heat and whisk in the remaining olive oil and white wine vinegar. Add salt and pepper to taste.

4. Toss the carrot slices and cooked prawns with the warm garlic rosemary dressing. Chill for at least 4 hours then serve cool or room temperature. Garnish with fresh parsley.

Serves 6

Pasta Shells with Prawn and Tomato Sauce

INGREDIENTS

185mL/6^1/2fl oz olive oil

2 cloves garlic, halved

3 x 440g/15^1/2oz cans peeled tomatoes, drained, seeded

2 tablespoons finely chopped parsley

salt

freshly ground black pepper

225g/8oz uncooked prawns, shelled, deveined and tails left intact

500g/1lb pasta shells

METHOD

1. Cook oil and garlic in a heavy-based saucepan, over moderate heat until garlic is brown. Discard garlic.

2. Add tomatoes to hot oil. Simmer about 8 minutes, breaking up tomatoes with a wooden spoon. The sauce should stay lumpy. Add parsley, season to taste with salt and pepper.

3. Add prawns to tomato sauce, stir over heat until prawns change colour, keep warm.

4. Cook pasta shells in boiling salted water until al dente. Drain. Place in a heated bowl. Pour sauce over pasta shells, toss to coat well.

Serves 4

Prawns with Feta

INGREDIENTS

1 small onion, finely chopped

15g/^{1}/2 oz butter

1 tablespoon olive oil

125mL/4fl oz dry white wine

4 tomatoes, peeled, seeded and chopped

1 clove garlic, crushed

^{3}/4 teaspoon chopped fresh oregano

salt

freshly ground black pepper

125g/4oz feta cheese, crumbled

1kg/2 lb uncooked prawns, peeled and deveined

4 tablespoons chopped fresh parsley

METHOD

1. Sauté onion in butter and olive oil in a saucepan for 5 minutes. Add wine, tomatoes, garlic and oregano. Season.

2. Bring to the boil, then simmer until sauce thickens slightly. Add cheese, mix well, then simmer for 10 minutes stirring occasionally.

3. Add prawns and cook over moderate heat for 5 minutes or until tender. Do not overcook. Transfer to a serving dish, sprinkle with parsley.

Serves 4

Prawns with Spinach

INGREDIENTS

100mL/3^1/2fl oz olive oil

1 onion, diced

1 red capsicum (pepper), seeded and diced

1 clove garlic, crushed

2 tomatoes, peeled and diced

1 ^{1}/2 bunches English spinach, washed and
roughly chopped

2 tablespoons dry white wine

juice of 1 lemon

salt and freshly ground black pepper

500g/1 lb green prawns, shelled and
  deveined

lemon wedges (to garnish)

METHOD

1. Heat 2 tablespoons of the olive oil in a
saucepan and brown the onion. Add the red
capsicum (pepper), garlic and tomatoes, and
cook for 7 minutes. Add the spinach, white
wine, lemon juice and seasoning.

2. Cover and simmer gently for 8-10 minutes
(until the spinach is tender). Take off the heat.
Stir and keep warm.

3. Add the remaining oil to a large frying pan.
Once hot, add the prawns and sauté, stirring
constantly, for 3 minutes, or until just cooked.

4. Spoon the prawns into the spinach, fold to
combine, and spoon onto a warm serving platter
and garnish with lemon wedges.

Serves 4

5

Linguine with Prawns and Scallops in a Roasted Tomato Sauce

INGREDIENTS

400g/14oz linguine

1kg/2 lb tomatoes

olive oil (small quantity/to drizzle over tomatoes)

salt and pepper

85mL/3oz olive oil (in addition to above)

200g/7oz scallops

200g/7oz green prawns, peeled

150g/5^{1}/$_{4}$oz calamari, cut into rings

200g/7oz firm white fish pieces

3 garlic cloves, crushed

2 brown onions, diced

1 tablespoon tomato paste (optional)

85mL/3oz water

^{1}/$_{2}$ bunch parsley, chopped

Parmesan cheese

METHOD

1. Cook the linguine in salted boiling water until al dente and set aside.

2. To roast the tomatoes: preheat the oven to 180°C/350°F. Cut the tomatoes in half and place on a baking tray. Drizzle with olive oil, sprinkle with a little salt and pepper, and roast in the oven for 20–25 minutes.

3. Place in a food processor and process for a few seconds, but do not over-process. (The mixture should still have texture.)

4. Heat half the oil in a pan, and sauté the scallops and the prawns for 2 minutes until just cooked and remove from the pan. Add the calamari and cook for 2 minutes, before removing from the pan. Adding a little more oil if needed, sauté the fish for a few minutes until just cooked, and remove from the pan.

5. Heat the remaining oil, and sauté the garlic and onion for a few minutes until cooked. Add the tomato mixture, tomato paste and water, and simmer for 10 minutes. Carefully add the seafood to the sauce, season with salt and pepper, and mix through the chopped parsley.

6. Serve with the linguine and parmesan cheese.

Serves 4

Spanish Rice with Scampi and Prawn

Spanish Rice with Scampi and Prawns

INGREDIENTS

3 tablespoons olive oil

1 medium onion, finely chopped

2 fresh squid, cleaned and finely chopped

1 large ripe tomato, skinned and chopped

300g/10^1/2oz short grain rice

3 cups/675mL/24fl oz water

pinch saffron threads

salt and ground pepper, to taste

8-16 fresh or thawed frozen scampi

500g/1lb fresh green king prawns

METHOD

1. In a large, heavy, flameproof, deep frying pan heat the oil and gently fry the chopped onion and squid for about 5 minutes. Add the tomato and cook for further 5 minutes.

2. Add rice and stir to mix well with the squid mixture for a minute or two. Bring water to boil with the saffron, salt and ground pepper, pour over the rice.

2. Add the shellfish, leaving the scampi either whole or halved and shelling the prawns or leaving them whole and unshelled.

3. Simmer over gentle heat until rice is cooked. The rice should not be stirred at all during the cooking so that the shellfish sits on top.

Serves 4

Spaghetti Marinara

INGREDIENTS

500g/1 lb spaghetti
2 teaspoons vegetable oil
2 teaspoons butter
2 onions, chopped
2 x 440g/15^1/2oz canned tomatoes,
** undrained and mashed**
2 tablespoons chopped fresh basil or
1 teaspoon dried basil
55mL/2fl oz dry white wine
12 mussels, scrubbed and beards removed
12 scallops
12 uncooked prawns, shelled and deveined
125g/4oz calamari (squid) rings

METHOD

1. Cook pasta in boiling water in a large saucepan following packet directions. Drain, set aside and keep warm.

2. Heat oil and butter in a frying pan over a medium heat. Add onions and cook, stirring, for 4 minutes or until onions are golden.

3. Stir in tomatoes, basil and wine, bring to simmering and simmer for 8 minutes. Add mussels, scallops and prawns and cook for 2 minutes longer.

4. Add calamari (squid) and cook for 1 minute or until shellfish is cooked. Spoon shellfish mixture over hot pasta and serve immediately.

Serves 4

Prawns with Garlic and Rosemary

INGREDIENTS

500g/1 lb green prawns, shelled and
** deveined**
2 cloves garlic, crushed
3 tablespoons olive oil
^{1}/4 teaspoon ground black pepper
2 sprigs fresh rosemary
3 tablespoons butter
^{1}/2 cup/115mL/4fl oz dry vermouth

METHOD

1. In a large bowl, combine the prawns, garlic, olive oil, pepper and rosemary, toss well. Cover and allow to marinate in the refrigerator for 8 hours or overnight.

2. In a large frying pan, melt the butter over high heat, add the prawns and marinate and saute until pink, about 2 minutes.

3. Transfer prawns to a bowl with a slotted spoon. Discard rosemary sprigs. Pour the vermouth into the frying pan, bring to the boil and reduce to a moderately thick consistency.

4. Return prawns to the sauce and toss in the glaze. Spoon prawns into serving dish and serve immediately.

Serves 4

Spaghetti Marinara

Prawns with Garlic and Rosemary

Spicy Prawns with Sun-dried Tomatoes

INGREDIENTS
3 tablespoons olive oil

1kg/2 lb green king prawns, peeled, deveined, tails intact

1 tablespoon tomato paste

2 teaspoon brown sugar

2 cloves garlic, crushed

1 tablespoon chilli sauce

1 tablespoon coriander, chopped

180g/6^1/2oz sun-dried tomatoes, drained

1 tablespoon fresh lime juice

snowpea sprouts, for garnish

METHOD
1. Heat the oil in a frying pan over moderate heat. Add the prawns and cook for 1 minute each side. Remove prawns with a slotted spoon and set aside.

2. Add the tomato paste, sugar, garlic, chilli sauce and coriander to frying pan and cook for 1 minute.

3. Return prawns to frying pan, add sun-dried tomatoes, toss in chilli sauce and sprinkle with lime juice. Place prawns on to a serving plate.

4. Garnish with snowpea sprouts and serve.

Serves 4

5

Pasta with Lobster and Prawns

INGREDIENTS

500g/1 lb small pasta shells
225g/8oz cooked prawns, shelled
1 cooked lobster
lemon juice
1 onion, chopped
2 cloves garlic, crushed
butter
1 cup/225g/8oz fresh tomato purée
1 tablespoon tomato paste
¹/2 cup/110mL/4fl oz white wine
³/4 cup/170mL/6fl oz cream
parsley

METHOD

1. Sprinkle shelled prawns with lemon and chill. After cleaning and shelling lobster, slice into rounds, sprinkle with lemon juice.

2. Take a frying pan and cook the onion and garlic in butter. Combine tomato purée and pasta with wine and add to onion mixture.

3. Simmer and when sauce is thickened, add cream, stirring well. Add seafood to the hot sauce. When thoroughly heated serve with cooked pasta. Garnish with parsley.

Serves 6

Italian Bouillabaisse

INGREDIENTS

500g/1 lb linguine or spaghetti
5 garlic cloves, bruised
1 cup/225ml/8fl oz olive oil
450g/16oz can tomatoes
3 cups/675mL/24fl oz of fish or
  vegetable stock
2 tablespoons parsley, chopped
2 tablespoons tarragon, chopped
salt and ground pepper
2 squid, cleaned and cut into rings
500g/1 lb white fish fillets
225g/8oz green prawns, shelled
225g/8oz scallops
12 mussels
12 each pippis, clams or any other
  molluscs available

METHOD

1. In a large skillet or heavy based saucepan, heat the oil and add the garlic cloves. Sauté gently until golden.

2. Add the fish stock and the roughly chopped tomatoes with their juice, parsley, tarragon and salt and pepper.

3. Bring the stock to a rolling simmer and add the squid and their tentacles, cook for 2 minutes and add the fish. Cover the pan and allow the fish and squid to cook 5 minutes or until tender. Remove the fish and keep warm.

4. Bring the stock to a simmer and add the prawns, scallops, and shellfish or molluscs and shake and toss the pan over a brink flame until all are cooked and the mussels are open, discard any that don't open and remove the garlic.

5. Check the seasoning and return the fish to the pot. Allow the fish to warm through.

6. While cooking the fish bring 4 litres of water to the boil and add salt and the pasta. Cook until al dente and drain.

7. Place the pasta into a large serving bowl and pour over the fish soup, gently placing all the fish and shell fish over the top. Garnish with parsley and serve with crusty bread with rouille.

Serves 4-6

Pasta with Seafood Sauce

INGREDIENTS

1 onion, finely chopped

2 tablespoons oil

2 cloves garlic, crushed

2 x 425g/15oz cans peeled tomato pieces, drained, juice reserved, and chopped

salt, pepper

1 teaspoon sugar

$^{1}/_{2}$ teaspoon dried basil

225g/8oz prawns, shelled and deveined

225g/8oz scallops

1 cup/225mL/8fl oz white wine

2 tablespoons chopped parsley

500g/1 lb linguine

2 teaspoons butter

METHOD

1. In a heavy based saucepan, sauté onion in hot oil until transparent and soft; add garlic and suté another minute. Add tomatoes, 1 cup reserved tomato liquid, salt, pepper, sugar and basil. Simmer slowly, uncovered, for 20 minutes.

2. In another saucepan, simmer prawns and scallops in wine for 4 minutes. Add to tomato mixture, add parsley and simmer another 5 minutes.

3. Boil linguine in plenty of boiling salted water until al dente. Drain and place on a heated serving platter and spoon sauce over. Serve immediately.

Serves 4

Our last section is a selection of prawn dishes we know you will enjo
always enjoyed, often with requests for seconds.

Butterflied Prawns with Garlic, Chilli & Parsley

INGREDIENTS

1kg/2 lb (approx. 20 individuals) green
  prawns, shelled. de-veined, tails intact
2 tablespoons olive oil
1 tablespoon lemon juice
2 cloves garlic, crushed
2 red chillies, seeded and finely chopped
2 tablespoons parsley, chopped
$^1/_2$ cup/55g/2oz flour
oil (for frying)
lemon (to garnish)

METHOD

1. Cut prawns down the back and remove vein.

2. Combine oil, lemon juice, garlic, chilli and parsley in a bowl. Add prawns, mix well, and leave to marinate for 2–3 hours.

3. Heat oil in a large pan, coat prawns with flour, and cook quickly in oil for 2–3 minutes. Drain on absorbent paper.

4. Serve with lemon wedges and parsley.

Serves 6

Potted Prawns

INGREDIENTS

185g/6$^1/_2$oz butter
500g/1lb uncooked peeled prawns, cut
  into small pieces
$^1/_2$ teaspoon ground mixed spice
$^1/_2$ teaspoon each freshly grated mace
and nutmeg
pinch cayenne pepper
freshly ground black pepper
hot toast points or melba toast to serve

METHOD

1. Melt butter in a frying pan over moderate heat until foaming subsides. Add prawns and spices, seasoning to taste, and cook, stirring, for 2-3 minutes or until prawns are pink and cooked.

2. Spoon mixture into four individual serving pots, pressing lightly. Cover prawns with rounds of aluminium foil then with a lid or extra foil and refrigerate for 2-3 hours or until firm. Serve with toast.

Serves 4

favourites as prawn tacos, prawn and pineapple curry and garlic prawns are

Butterflied Prawns with Garlic, Chilli & Parsley

Prawn Jambalaya

INGREDIENTS

3 rashers bacon, cut into strips
1 large onion, finely chopped
1 green pepper, diced
1 stalk celery, chopped
3 cloves garlic, crushed
1 cup/220g/7oz long-grain rice
375-500mL/13^1/4-17^1/2fl oz boiling
  chicken stock
440g/15^1/2oz canned tomatoes, drained and
  mashed
2 teaspoons Cajun spice mix
1 teaspoon dried thyme
500g/1lb uncooked medium prawns, shelled
  and deveined
155g/5^1/2oz smoked ham in one piece, cut
  into 1cm/^{1}/2 in cubes
3 spring onions, finely chopped

METHOD

1. Cook bacon in a frying pan over a medium heat for 5 minutes or until crisp. Remove bacon from pan and drain on absorbent kitchen paper.

2. Add onion to pan and cook, stirring, for 5 minutes or until onion is soft, but not brown. Add green pepper, celery and garlic and cook for 3 minutes. Add rice and cook, stirring frequently, for 5 minutes or until rice becomes translucent.

3. Stir in stock, tomatoes, spice mix and thyme and bring to the boil. Cover, reduce heat to low and cook for 15 minutes. Stir in prawns and ham, cover and cook for 10 minutes longer or until rice is tender and liquid absorbed. Sprinkle with spring onions and serve immediately.

Serves 4

Prawn Tostaditas

INGREDIENTS

vegetable oil
8 corn tortillas
1/2 avocado, chopped
2 tablespoons shredded fresh mint
<u>Prawn and Vegetable Topping</u>
1 cob sweet corn
1 red capsicum (pepper), quartered
1 yellow capsicum (pepper), quartered
1 red onion, cut into wedges
375g/13^1/4oz medium uncooked prawns,
  shelled and deveined
4 mild fresh green chillies, cut
  into strips
1 tablespoon lime juice

METHOD

1. To make topping, place sweet corn cob and red and yellow capsicum (peppers) on a preheated hot barbecue or char-grill and cook until lightly charred. Cut corn from cob and set aside. Cut capsicums (peppers) into strips and set aside.

2. Heat 2 teaspoons of oil in a frying pan over a medium heat, add onion and cook for 4 minutes or until golden. Add prawns, chillies and lime juice and cook for 2 minutes or until prawns change colour. Add sweet corn kernels and red and yellow capsicums (peppers), toss to combine and set aside.

3. Heat 2^1/2cm/1 in oil in a frying pan over a medium heat until a cube of bread dropped in browns in 50 seconds. Cook tortillas, one at time, for 45 seconds each side or until crisp. Drain on absorbent kitchen paper.

4. To serve, pile topping onto tortillas, then scatter with avocado and mint. Serve immediately.

Serves 4

Shrimp Creole

INGREDIENTS

1/4 cup/55mL/2fl oz olive oil
1 large onion, finely chopped
1 green capsicum (pepper)
1 large stalk celery
4 large rip tomatoes, peeled and chopped
500mL/17¹/2fl oz fish stock (or prawn
  stock made from heads and shells from
  prawns)
salt and freshly ground pepper
pinch cayenne
bouquet garni
1kg/2 lb green prawns, shelled
chopped parsley

METHOD

1. Heat oil in large heavy frypan and sauté prawns, green capsicum (pepper) and celery for a few minutes until softened. Add chopped tomatoes, fish stock, salt, pepper, cayenne and bouquet garni. Bring to simmer and cook for about 25 minutes.

2. Scoop away the vegetables and set aside, leaving the liquid in the pan. Reduce theliquid over a moderate heat to about half, then return vegetables along with the prawns.

3. Simmer for about 5 minutes, remove bouquet garni and serve sprinkled with chopped parsely.

Yucateco Seafood Risotto

INGREDIENTS

500g/1 lb assorted seafood such as
  prawns, calamari and scallops
500g/1 lb white fish fillets (no bones)
  such as blue eye
2 tablespoons olive oil
1/4-1/2 teaspoon minced chilli
2 cloves garlic, crushed
1 tablespoon olive oil
2 onions, sliced
400g/14oz arborio rice
200mL/7fl oz white wine
700mL/25fl oz rich fish stock,
  simmering
2 bay leaves
1/2 cup/115mL/4fl oz milk or hot taco
  sauce
2 ribs celery, sliced
2 large tomatoes, chopped
2 potatoes, peeled and diced
100mL/3¹/2oz cream
1 bunch parsley, chopped
1 teaspoon paprika
2 potatoes, boiled and thinly sliced

METHOD

1. Prepare the shellfish. Cut the fish fillets into 2¹/2cm/1 in chunks and rinse the shellfish. Heat the olive oil and sauté the garlic, chilli and fish chunks until opaque. Remove with a slotted spoon and keep warm. Add the shellfish to the same pan and sauté until just cooked and changed colour, about 3 minutes. Remove the pan from the heat, return the fish and mix gently. Set aside.

2. In a large saucepan, heat the olive oil and sauté the onions. Add the rice and stir to coat, allowing the rice to become translucent. Add the wine and allow to simmer until the liquid evaporates. Add the bay leaves, potato cubes and celery with the first addition of half a cup of stock. Stir vigorously to combine. When the stock has been absorbed, add the next half cup of stock. Continue in this fashion, adding stock and stirring thoroughly until the last quantity of stock is to be added.

3. At this time, add the chopped tomatoes, taco sauce, cream and half the parsley. When all the ingredients have been added and most of the stock has been absorbed, remove the pan from the heat, remove the bay leaves and serve in individual bowls on a bed of boiled sliced potatoes, garnished with plenty of parsley and a sprinkling of paprika.

Serves 6

Yucateco Seafood Risotto

6

Seafood with Green Vegetables

Seafood with Green Vegetables

INGREDIENTS

100g/3^1/2 oz snow peas (mangetout)
225g/8oz broccoli, broken into small
  florets
225g/8oz asparagus spears, trimmed
370mL/13fl oz fish stock
225g/8oz large uncooked prawns, shelled
  and deveined, tails intact
225g/8oz firm white fish fillets, cut into 2
  cm/^{3}/4 in cubes
225g/8oz scallops
1/2 cup/115mL/4fl oz cream (double)
1/4 cup/55mL/2fl oz tomato purée
1 tablespoon chopped fresh tarragon or 1
  teaspoon dried tarragon
freshly ground black pepper

METHOD

1. Steam or microwave snow peas
(mangetout), broccoli and asparagus,
separately, until just tender. Drain, refresh
under cold running water and set aside.

2. Place stock in a large saucepan and bring to
the boil, add prawns, fish and scallops to stock
and cook for 5 minutes or until just cooked.
Using a slotted spoon, remove and set aside.

3. Stir in cream, tomato purée and tarragon
and bring to the boil. Reduce heat and simmer
for 10 minutes or until liquid is reduced by one-
third. Add reserved vegetables and seafood to
sauce and cook for 1-2 minutes or until heated
through. Season to taste with black pepper and
serve immediately.

Serves 4

Prawns in Peppercorn Sauce

INGREDIENTS

3 tablespoons butter
5 tablespoons flour
2 cups/450mL/16fl oz milk
1 cup/225mL/8fl oz chicken stock
pinch ground cayenne pepper
^{1}/2 teaspoon dry mustard
2 tablespoons sherry
^{1}/2 cup/115mL/4fl oz cream
1 tablespoon canned green peppercorns
  (rinsed)
2kg/4 lb cooked medium king prawns
  (peeled and deveined)

METHOD

1. Heat butter in a large saucepan, stir in
flour, and cook (stirring) for 2 minutes.

2. Over low heat, gradually stir in milk and
stock, cook (stirring continuously) until
mixture thickens and boils.

3. Add cayenne, mustard, sherry, cream,
peppercorns and prawns. Simmer gently until
prawns are heated through.

Serves 6

Almond Crumbed Prawns

INGREDIENTS

750g/1^1/2 lb green king prawns
65g/2^1/4oz plain flour
1 egg
85mL/3fl oz milk
225g/8oz almonds (blanched)
oil (for deep frying)

METHOD

1. Shell prawns (leaving tails intact, but
remove vein). Cut prawns down back, and
spread out flat.

2. Sift flour into basin, make a well in the
centre, add combined beaten egg and milk,
and gradually stir in flour. Beat until smooth.

3. Dip prawns into batter, and then roll in
finely chopped almonds.

4. Drop into hot oil, and fry until golden
brown.

Serves 4–6

Prawn and Pineapple Curry

INGREDIENTS

500g/1lb green king prawns, shelled and deveined

1 stalk lemongrass, roughly chopped

5 spring onions, peeled

3 cloves garlic, peeled

4 fresh red chillies, halved and seeded

1 teaspoon ground turmeric

3 tablespoons chopped coriander (celantro)

6 tablespoons vegetable oil

$^1/_2$ teaspoon shrimp paste

1 can coconut milk

1 can sliced pineapple

salt, to taste

METHOD

1. Using a blender or food processor grind the lemongrass with the spring onions, garlic, chillies , turmeric and coriander.

2. Heat the oil in a wok and add the ground paste. Cook for a minute then stir in shrimp paste with the thin part of the coconut milk. When mixture is bubbling stir in the prawns and the remaining coconut milk.

3. Allow to heat for a few minutes then stir in drained, sliced pineapple pieces and continue to simmer for about 10 minutes. Serve with steamed rice.

Serves 4

Baked Mushrooms Stuffed with Prawns

INGREDIENTS

4 tablespoons vegetable oil

1 small carrot, cut into julienne strips

1 stalk celery, cut into julienne strips

1/2 leek or onion, cut into julienne strips

8 large open cup mushrooms, stems removed

115g/4oz butter

500g/1lb green prawns, shelled and de-veined, tails intact

4 cloves garlic, crushed

salt

freshly ground black pepper

4 tablespoon chopped fresh parsley

3 tablespoon fresh lemon juice

METHOD

1. Heat oil in a frying pan over moderate heat and cook carrot, celery and leek or onion, stirring, until cooked but still crisp. Using a slotted spoon, remove vegetables to a plate. Add mushrooms to pan and cook, stirring, for 1 minute each side. Arrange mushrooms in a baking dish. Preheat oven to 180°C/350°F/Gas 4.

2. Melt butter in frying pan over moderate heat until foaming subsides, add prawns and garlic and cook, stirring, until pink and cooked. Add parsley and lemon juice to pan, season to taste with salt and black pepper and heat through, stirring. Remove pan from heat. Reserve a few prawns for garnish.

3. Cut remaining prawns into small pieces, arrange in mushroom caps and bake for 4-6 minutes or until heated through and bubbly. Return vegetables to frying pan, season to taste with salt and black pepper and heat through.

4. To serve, arrange 2 mushrooms on each heated entrée plate, spoon vegetables onto plates, garnish with reserved prawns and serve immediately.

This robust dish is well-flavoured with garlic.

Serves 4

Mexican Prawns with Salsa

INGREDIENTS

750g/1¹/₂ lb uncooked large prawns, shelled and deveined
2 tablespoons lime juice
2 teaspoons ground cumin
2 tablespoons chopped fresh coriander (cilantro)
2 fresh red chillies, chopped
2 teaspoons vegetable oil
4 tortillas or flat bread
Avocado Salsa
1 avocado, stoned, peeled and chopped
1 tablespoon lemon juice
¹/₂ red capsicum (pepper), chopped
2 spring onions, chopped
¹/₂ teaspoon chilli powder
1 tablespoon fresh coriander (cilantro) leaves

METHOD

1. Place prawns, lime juice, cumin, chopped coriander (cilantro), chillies and oil in a bowl, toss to combine and set aside to marinate for 5 minutes.

2. To make salsa, place avocado, lemon juice, red capsicum (pepper), spring onions, chilli powder and coriander (cilantro) leaves in a bowl and mix gently to combine. Set aside.

3. Heat a nonstick frying pan over a high heat, add prawns and stir-fry for 4-5 minutes or until prawns are cooked. To serve, divide prawns between tortillas or flat bread and top with salsa.
Serves 4

Prawn Ceviche

INGREDIENTS

500g/1lb medium green prawns, shelled and deveined
³/₄ cup/170mL/6fl oz lime juice
³/₄ cup/170mL/6fl oz lemon juice
¹/₂ cup/115mL/4fl oz orange juice
1 fresh hot chilli, cut into strips
1 clove garlic, crushed
1 teaspoon brown sugar
1 red capsicum (pepper), cut into strips
¹/₂ small red onion, cut into strips
2 tablespoons fresh coriander (cilantro), chopped
2 ripe tomatoes, seeded and diced
salt and ground black pepper

METHOD

1. In a bowl, marinate prawns in a mixture of the citrus juices, chilli, garlic and sugar for at least 6 hours or overnight. This marinade will 'cold cook' the prawns. The prawns should lose their translucent appearance.

2. Remove prawns from marinade and toss with remaining ingredients, seasoning well with salt and freshly ground black pepper.

King Prawns in a Sweet Potato Crust

INGREDIENTS

For Prawns

500g/1 lb large raw prawns, peeled and de-veined

2 spring onions, finely chopped

1 stalk lemon grass, finely chopped

1 tablespoons fresh ginger, minced

1/2 bunch fresh coriander (cilantro), finely chopped

1 teaspoon fish sauce

1 tablespoons sweet chilli sauce

2 tablespoons peanut oil

For Batter

300g/10¹/₂oz kumara (sweet potato)

1/2 teaspoon turmeric

1 cup/225mL/8fl oz coconut milk

1/2 cup/115mL/4fl oz water

1/2 cup/55g/2oz self-raising flour

1/2 cup/55g/2oz rice flour

1 tablespoon polenta

METHOD

1. Chop the prawns roughly and mix with all the finely chopped spring onions, lemon grass, fresh ginger, coriander (cilantro), fish sauce and sweet chilli sauce. Allow to marinate for 1 hour.

2. Meanwhile, grate the kumara. In a separate bowl, mix the turmeric, coconut milk, water, self-raising flour, rice-flour and polenta. Stir thoroughly to combine, then add the grated kumara and set aside until prawns are ready. Combine the prawn mixture with the batter and mix thoroughly.

3. Heat a non-stick frypan with peanut oil and drop tablespoons of the prawn mixture into the frypan. Cook over a medium-high heat for three minutes on each side, or until the underside is crisp and golden. Turn them over and cook the other side.

4. When cooked, remove the fritters from the frypan. Allow them to cool on a wire rack, or serve immediately with lime wedges. To reheat, place the wire rack in the oven (preheated to 200°C/400°F) for 5–10 minutes.
Variation: If you do not wish to use shellfish, substitute fresh salmon for the prawns and dice before mixing with the marinade ingredients. Then proceed with the recipe above. A combination of prawns and salmon also works very well.

Makes 12-16 fritters

KING PRAWNS I
SWEE

OTATO CRUST

Prawns with Garlic and Wine Sauce

INGREDIENTS
55mL/2fl oz olive oil
6 cloves garlic, crushed
1/2 bunch parsley, chopped
1 bay leaf
1 red chilli, chopped
1kg/2 lb green prawns, shelled and deveined
1/2 cup/115mL/4fl oz dry white wine
salt and black pepper to taste

METHOD
1. Heat oil and cook garlic over medium heat for 2 minutes.

2. Add the parsley, bay leaf, chilli and prawns and cook over high heat for 2 minutes more.

3. Add the wine and cook for another 3 minutes until the prawns are cooked and the wine has reduced to about half. Season with salt and pepper.

Serves 3-4

6

Prawn Empanadas

INGREDIENTS
vegetable oil for deep-frying
Empanada Dough
2 3/4 cups/350g/12 1/4oz flour
55g/2oz soft butter
3/4 cup/170mL/6fl oz warm water
Chilli and Prawn Filling
2 teaspoons vegetable oil
1 onion, chopped
1 tablespoon fresh oregano leaves
2 teaspoons fresh lemon thyme leaves
500g/1 lb peeled uncooked prawns
2 green tomatoes, peeled and chopped
4 poblano chillies, roasted, seeded and peeled and chopped
5 button mushrooms, thinly sliced
1/4 lettuce, shredded
2 spring onions, thinly sliced

METHOD
1. To make dough, place flour and butter in a food processor and process until mixture resembles coarse breadcrumbs. With machine running, add enough of the warm water to form a smooth dough. Knead dough on a lightly floured surface for 3 minutes, then divide into 12 portions. Cover with a damp cloth and set aside.

2. To make filling, heat oil in a frying pan over medium heat, add onion, oregano and thyme and cook for 4 minutes or until onions are golden. Add prawns, tomatoes and chillies and simmer for 5 minutes or until mixture reduces and thickens. Cool.

3. Roll each portion of dough out to form an 18 cm/7 in circle about 3 mm/1/8 in thick. Place 3 tablespoons of filling on one half of each dough round, then fold over to enclose filling and pinch edges to seal.

4. Heat oil in a saucepan until a cube of bread dropped in browns in 50 seconds, then cook empanadas, a few at a time, for 2-3 minutes or until crisp and golden. Drain on absorbent kitchen paper and serve.

Makes 12

Prawn Tacos

INGREDIENTS

8 flour tortillas, warmed
155g/5^1/2oz feta cheese crumbled
<u>**Seafood Filling**</u>
2 teaspoons vegetable oil
1 onion, chopped
2 tomatoes, chopped
375g/13^1/2oz white fish, cubed
225g/8oz shelled and deveined
  medium uncooked prawns
12 scallops
3 medium fresh green chillies, chopped
2 tablespoons chopped fresh oregano
1 teaspoon finely grated lemon rind

METHOD

1. To make filling, heat oil in a frying pan over a high heat, add onion and cook for 4 minutes or until golden. Add tomatoes and cook for 5 minutes. Add fish, prawns, scallops, chillies, oregano and lemon rind and cook, tossing, for 3-4 minutes or until seafood is cooked.

2. To serve, spoon filling down the centre of each tortilla and scatter with feta cheese. Fold tortilla to enclose filling and serve immediately.

Serves 4

Peppered Prawns

INGREDIENTS

750g/1¹/₂ lb green king prawns

1 small chicken stock cube

2 teaspoons cornflour

115mL/4fl oz water

2 tablespoons soy sauce

1 tablespoon dry sherry

2 tablespoons tomato sauce

1 clove garlic, crushed

2 teaspoons cracked black peppercorns

1 tablespoon honey

2 tablespoons oil

500g/1 lb broccoli, cut into flowerets

425g/15oz can baby corn, drained

1 onion, sliced

1 stick celery, thinly sliced

1 red capsicum (pepper), thinly sliced

cornflour (extra)

1 tablespoon water (extra)

METHOD

1. Peel and devein prawns (leaving tails intact). Mix together the chicken stock cube, cornflour and water, and set aside.

2. Combine soy sauce, sherry, tomato sauce, garlic, pepper and honey in a large dish. Add prawns, cover, and refrigerate for several hours.

3. Heat oil in wok or large frying pan. Add vegetables, and stir-fry for about 2 minutes.

4. Add prawns and marinade to pan, and cook (stirring) over high heat until prawns change colour and are cooked.

5. Stir in extra cornflour, combined with extra water, and cook stirring until smooth.

Serves 4–6

WEIGHTS & MEASURES

Cooking is not an exact science: one does not require finely calibrated scales, pipettes and scientific equipment to cook, yet the conversion to metric measures in some countries and its interpretations must have intimidated many a good cook.

Weights are given in the recipes only for ingredients such as meats, fish, poultry and some vegetables. Though a few grams/ounces one way or another will not affect the success of your dish.

Though recipes have been tested using the Australian Standard 250mL cup, 20mL tablespoon and 5mL teaspoon, they will work just as well with the US and Canadian 8fl oz cup, or the UK 300mL cup. We have used graduated cup measures in preference to tablespoon measures so that proportions are always the same. Where tablespoon measures have been given, these are not crucial measures, so using the smaller tablespoon of the US or UK will not affect the recipe's success. At least we all agree on the teaspoon size. For breads, cakes and pastries, the only area which might cause concern is where eggs are used, as proportions will then vary. If working with a 250mL or 300mL cup, use large eggs (65g/21/4 oz), adding a little more liquid to the recipe for 300mL cup measures if it seems necessary. Use the medium-sized eggs (55g/2oz) with 8fl oz cup measure. A graduated set of measuring cups and spoons is recommended, the cups in particular for measuring dry ingredients. Remember to level such ingredients to ensure their accuracy.

English Measures

All measurements are similar to Australian with two exceptions: the English cup measures 300mL/10fl oz, whereas the Australian cup measure 250mL/8fl oz. The English tablespoon (the Australian dessertspoon) measures 14.8mL/1/2fl oz against the Australian tablespoon of 20mL/3/4fl oz.

American Measures

The American reputed pint is 16fl oz, a quart is equal to 32fl oz and the American gallon, 128fl oz. The Imperial measurement is 20fl oz to the pint, 40fl oz a quart and 160fl oz one gallon. The American tablespoon is equal to 14.8mL/$1/2$ fl oz, the teaspoon is 5mL/$1/6$ fl oz. The cup measure is 250mL/8fl oz, the same as Australia.

Dry Measures

All the measures are level, so when you have filled a cup or spoon, level it off with the edge of a knife. The scale below is the "cook's equivalent"; it is not an exact conversion of metric to imperial measurement. To calculate the exact metric equivalent yourself, use 2.2046 lb = 1kg or 1 lb = 0.45359kg

Metric	Imperial	
g = grams	oz = ounces	
kg = kilograms	lb = pound	
15g	1/2oz	
20g	2/3oz	
30g	1oz	
55g	2oz	
85g	3oz	
115g	4oz	1/
140g	5oz	
170g	6oz	
200g	7oz	
225g	8oz	1/
315g	11oz	
340g	12oz	3/
370g	13oz	
400g	14oz	
425g	15oz	
455g	16oz	
1,000g	1kg 35.2oz	2
1.5kg	3.3 lb	

WEIGHTS & MEASURES

The Celsius temperatures given here are not exact; they have been rounded off and are given as a guide only. Follow the manufacturer's temperature guide, relating it to oven description given in the recipe. Remember gas ovens are hottest at the top, electric ovens at the bottom and convection-fan forced ovens are usually even throughout. We included Regulo numbers for gas cookers which may assist.
To convert °C to °F multiply °C by 9 and divide by 5 then add 32.

Oven temperatures

	C°	F°	Regular
Very slow	120	250	1
Slow	150	300	2
Moderately slow	160	325	3
Moderate	180	350	4
Moderately hot	190-200	370-400	5-6
Hot	210-220	410-440	6-7
Very hot	230	450	8
Super hot	250-290	475-500	9-10

Cake dish sizes

Metric	Imperial
15cm	6in
18cm	7in
20cm	8in
23cm	9in

Loaf dish sizes

Metric	Imperial
23x12cm	9x5in
25x8cm	10x3in
28x18cm	11x7in

Liquid measures

Metric mL millilitres	Imperial fl oz fluid ounce	Cup & Spoon
5mL	$1/6$ fl oz	1 teaspoon
20mL	$2/3$ fl oz	1 tablespoon
30mL	1fl oz	(1 tablespoon (plus 2 teaspoons

55mL	2fl oz	$1/4$ cup
85mL	3fl oz	$1/3$ cup
115mL	4fl oz	$3/8$ cup
125mL	$4^1/2$fl oz	$1/2$ cup
150mL	$5^1/4$fl oz	$1/4$ pint, 1 gill
225mL	8fl oz	1 cup
300mL	$10^1/2$fl oz	$1/2$ pint
370mL	13fl oz	$1^1/2$ cups
400mL	14fl oz	$1^3/4$ cups
455mL	16fl oz	2 cups
570mL	20fl oz	1 pint, $2^1/2$ cups
1 litre	35fl oz	1 $2/4$ pints, 4 cups

Cup measurements

One cup is equal to the following weights.

	Metric	Imperial
Almonds, flaked	85g	3oz
Almonds, slivered, ground	125g	$4^1/2$oz
Almonds, kernel	155g	$5^1/2$oz
Apples, dried, chopped	125g	$4^1/2$oz
Apricots, dried, chopped	190g	$6^3/4$oz
Breadcrumbs, packet	125g	$4^1/2$oz
Breadcrumbs, soft	55g	2oz
Cheese, grated	115g	4oz
Choc bits	155g	$5^1/2$oz
Coconut, desiccated	85g	3oz
Cornflakes	30g	1oz
Currants	155g	$5^1/2$oz
Flour	115g	4oz
Fruit, dried (mixed, sultanas etc)	170g	6oz
Ginger, crystallised, glace	225g	8oz
Honey, treacle, golden syrup	315g	11oz
Mixed peel	225g	8oz
Nuts, chopped	115g	4oz
Prunes, chopped	225g	7oz
Rice, cooked	155g	5oz
Rice, uncooked	225g	8oz
Rolled oats	85g	3oz
Sesame seeds	115g	4oz
Shortening (butter, margarine)	225g	8oz
Sugar, brown	155g	$5^1/2$oz
Sugar, granulated or caster	225g	8oz
Sugar, sifted icing	155g	$5^1/2$oz
Wheatgerm	55g	2oz

Length

Some of us still have trouble converting imperial length to metric. In this scale, measures have been rounded off to the easiest-to-use and most acceptable figures.
To obtain the exact metric equivalent in converting inches to centimetres, multiply inches by 2.54 whereby 1 inch equals 25.4 millimetres and 1 millimetre equals 0.03937 inches.

Metric mm=millimetres cm=centimetres	Imperial in = inches ft = feet
5mm, 0.5cm	$1/4$ in
10mm, 1.0cm	$1/2$ in
20mm, 2.0cm	$3/4$ in
2.5cm	1in
5cm	2in
8cm	3in
10cm	4in
12cm	5in
15cm	6in
18cm	7in
20cm	8in
23cm	9in
25cm	10in
28cm	11in
30cm	1 ft, 12in

GLOSSARY

acidulated water: water with added acid, such as lemon juice or vinegar, which prevents discoloration of ingredients, particularly fruit or vegetables. The proportion of acid to water is 1 teaspoon per 300ml.

al dente: Italian cooking term for ingredients that are cooked until tender but still firm to the bite; usually applied to pasta.

americaine: method of serving seafood - usually lobster and monkfish - in a sauce flavoured with olive oil, aromatic herbs, tomatoes, white wine, fish stock, brandy and tarragon.

anglaise: cooking style for simple cooked dishes such as boiled vegetables. Assiette anglaise is a plate of cold cooked meats.

antipasto: Italian for "before the meal", it denotes an assortment of cold meats, vegetables and cheeses, often marinated, served as an hors d'oeuvre. A typical antipasto might include salami, prosciutto, marinated artichoke hearts, anchovy fillets, olives, tuna fish and Provolone cheese.

au gratin: food sprinkled with breadcrumbs, often covered with cheese sauce and browned until a crisp coating forms.

balsamic vinegar: a mild, extremely fragrant wine-based vinegar made in northern Italy. Traditionally, the vinegar is aged for at least seven years in a series of casks made of various woods.

baste: to moisten food while it is cooking by spooning or brushing on liquid or fat.

baine marie: a saucepan standing in a large pan which is filled with boiling water to keep liquids at simmering point. A double boiler will do the same job.

beat: to stir thoroughly and vigorously.

beurre manie: equal quantities of butter and flour kneaded together and added a little at a time to thicken a stew or casserole.

bird: see paupiette.

blanc: a cooking liquid made by adding flour and lemon juice to water in order to keep certain vegetables from discolouring as they cook.

blanch: to plunge into boiling water and then in some cases, into cold water. Fruits and nuts are blanched to remove skin easily.

blanquette: a white stew of lamb, veal or chicken, bound with egg yolks and cream and accompanied by onion and mushrooms.

blend: to mix thoroughly.

bonne femme: dishes cooked in the traditional French "housewife" style. Chicken and pork bonne femme are garnished with bacon, potatoes and baby onion; fish bonne femme with mushrooms in a white wine sauce.

bouquet garni: a bunch of herbs, usually consisting of sprigs of parsley, thyme, marjoram, rosemary, a bay leaf, peppercorns and cloves, tied in muslin and used to flavour stews and casseroles.

braise: to cook whole or large pieces of poultry, game, fish, meat or vegetables in a small amount of wine, stock or other liquid in a closed pot. Often the main ingredient is first browned in fat and then cooked in a low oven or very slowly on top of the stove. Braising suits tough meats and older birds and produces a mellow, rich sauce.

broil: The American term for grilling food.

brown: cook in a small amount of fat until brown.

burghul (also bulgur): a type of cracked wheat, where the kernels are steamed and dried before being crushed.

buttered: to spread with softened or melted butter.

butterfly: to slit a piece of food in half horizontally, cutting it almost through so that when opened it resembles butterfly wings. Chops, large prawns and thick fish fillets are often butterflied so that they cook more quickly.

buttermilk: a tangy, low-fat cultured milk product whose slight acidity makes it an ideal marinade base for poultry.

calzone: a semicircular pocket of pizza dough, stuffed with meat or vegetables, sealed and baked.

caramelise: to melt sugar until it is a golden brown syrup.

champignons: small mushrooms, usually canned.

chasseur: (hunter) a French cooking style in which meat and chicken dishes are cooked with mushrooms, shallots, white wine, and often tomato.

clarify: to melt butter and drain the oil off the sediment.

coat: to cover with a thin layer of flour, sugar, nuts, crumbs, poppy or sesame seeds, cinnamon sugar or a few of the ground spices.

concasser: to chop coarsely, usually tomatoes.

confit: from the French verb confire, meaning to preserve. Food that is made into a preserve by cooking very slowly and thoroughly until tender. In the case of meat, such as duck or goose, it is cooked in its own fat, and covered with it so that it does not come into contact with the air. Vegetables such as onions are good inconfit.

consomme: a clear soup usually made from beef.

coulis: a thin puree, usually of fresh or cooked fruit or vegetables, which is soft enough to pour (couler means to run). A coulis may be rough-textured or very smooth.

court bouillon: the liquid in which fish, poultry or meat is cooked. It usually consists of water with bay leaf, onion, carrots and salt and freshly ground black pepper to taste. Other additives can include wine, vinegar, stock, garlic or spring onions (scallions).

couscous: cereal processed from semolina into pellets, traditionally steamed and served with meat and vegetables in the classic North African stew of the same name.

cruciferous vegetables: certain members of the mustard, cabbage and turnip families with cross-shaped flowers and strong aromas and flavours.

cream: to make soft, smooth and creamy by rubbing with back of spoon or by beating with mixer. Usually applied to fat and sugar.

croutons: small toasted or fried cubes of bread.

crudites: raw vegetables, whether cut in slices or sticks to nibble plain or with a dipping sauce, or shredded and tossed as salad with a simple dressing.

cube: to cut into small pieces with 6 equal sides.

curdle: to cause milk or sauce to separate into solid and liquid. Example, overcooked egg mixtures.

daikon radish (also called mooli): a long white Japanese

radish. dark sesame oil (also called Oriental sesame oil): dark polyunsaturated oil with a low burning point, used for seasoning. Do not replace with lighter sesame oil.

deglaze: to dissolve congealed cooking juices or glaze on the bottom of a pan by adding a liquid, then scraping and stirring vigorously whilst bringing the liquid to the boil. Juices may be used to make gravy or to add to sauce.

degrease: to skim grease from the surface of liquid. If possible the liquid should be chilled so the fat solidifies. If not, skim off most of the fat with a large metal spoon, then trail strips of paper towel on the surface of the liquid to remove any remaining globules.

devilled: a dish or sauce that is highly seasoned with a hot ingredient such as mustard, Worcestershire sauce or cayenne pepper.

dice: to cut into small cubes.

dietary fibre: a plant-cell material that is undigested or only partially digested in the human body, but which promotes healthy digestion of other food matter.

dissolve: mix a dry ingredient with liquid until absorbed.

dredge: to coat with a dry ingredient, as flour or sugar.

drizzle: to pour in a fine thread-like stream over a surface.

dust: to sprinkle or coat lightly with flour or icing sugar.

Dutch oven: a heavy casserole with a lid usually made from cast iron or pottery.

emulsion: a mixture of two liquids that are not mutually soluble - for example, oil and water.

entree: in Europe, the "entry" or hors d'oeuvre; in North America entree means the main course.

fillet: special cut of beef, lamb, pork or veal; breast of poultry and game; fish cut of the bone lengthways.

flake: to break into small pieces with a fork.

flame: to ignite warmed alcohol over food.

fold in: a gentle, careful combining of a light or delicate mixture with a heavier mixture using a metal spoon.

fricassee: a dish in which poultry, fish or vegetables are bound together with a white or veloute sauce. In Britain and the United States, the name applies to an old-fashioned dish of chicken in a creamy sauce.

galette: sweet or savoury mixture shaped as a flat round.

garnish: to decorate food, usually with something edible.

gastrique: caramelized sugar deglazed with vinegar and used in fruit-flavoured savoury sauces, in such dishes as duck with orange.

glaze: a thin coating of beaten egg, syrup or aspic which is brushed over pastry, fruits or cooked meats.

gluten: a protein in flour that is developed when dough is kneaded, making it elastic.

gratin: a dish cooked in the oven or under the grill so that it develops a brown crust. Breadcrumbs or cheese may be sprinkled on top first. Shallow gratin dishes ensure a maximum area of crust.

grease: to rub or brush lightly with oil or fat.

infuse: to immerse herbs, spices or other flavourings in hot liquid to flavour it. Infusion takes from two to five minutes depending on the flavouring. The liquid should be very hot but not boiling.

jardiniere: a garnish of garden vegetables, typically carrots, pickling onions, French beans and turnips.

GLOSSARY

joint: to cut poultry, game or small animals into serving pieces by dividing at the joint.

julienne: to cut food into match-like strips.

knead: to work dough using heel of hand with a pressing motion, while stretching and folding the dough.

lights: lungs of an animal, used in various meat preparations such as pates and faggots.

line: to cover the inside of a container with paper, to protect or aid in removing mixture.

macerate: to soak food in liquid to soften.

marinade: a seasoned liquid, usually an oil and acid mixture, in which meats or other foods are soaked to soften and give more flavour.

marinara: Italian "sailor's style" cooking that does not apply to any particular combination of ingredients. Marinara tomato sauce for pasta is most familiar.

marinate: to let food stand in a marinade to season and tenderize.

mask: to cover cooked food with sauce.

melt: to heat until liquified.

mince: to grind into very small pieces.

mix: to combine ingredients by stirring.

monounsaturated fats: one of three types of fats found in foods. Are believed not to raise the level of cholesterol in the blood.

nicoise: a garnish of tomatoes, garlic and black olives; a salad with anchovy, tuna and French beans is typical.

non-reactive pan: a cooking pan whose surface does not chemically react with food. Materials used include stainless steel, enamel, glass and some alloys.

noisette: small "nut" of lamb cut from boned loin or rack that is rolled, tied and cut in neat slices. Noisette also means flavoured with hazelnuts, or butter cooked to a nut brown colour.

normande: a cooking style for fish, with a garnish of shrimp, mussels and mushrooms in a white wine cream sauce; for poultry and meat, a sauce with cream, Calvados and apple.

olive oil: various grades of oil extract from olives. Extra virgin olive oil has a full, fruity flavour and the lowest acidity. Virgin olive oil is slightly higher in acidity and lighter in flavour. Pure olive oil is a processed blend of olive oils and has the highest acidity and lightest taste.

panade: a mixture for binding stuffings and dumplings, notably quenelles, often of choux pastry or simply breadcrumbs. A panade may also be made of frangipane, pureed potatoes or rice.

papillote: to cook food in oiled or buttered greasepoof paper or aluminium foil. Also a decorative frill to cover bone ends of chops and poultry drumsticks.

parboil: to boil or simmer until part cooked (i.e. cooked further than when blanching).

pare: to cut away outside covering.

pate: a paste of meat or seafood used as a spread for toast or crackers.

paupiette: a thin slice of meat, poultry or fish spread with a savoury stuffing and rolled. In the United States this is also called "bird" and in Britain an "olive".

peel: to strip away outside covering.

plump: to soak in liquid or moisten thoroughly until full and round.

poach: to simmer gently in enough hot liquid to cover, using care to retain shape of food.

polyunsaturated fat: one of the three types of fats found in food. These exist in large quantities in such vegetable oils as safflower, sunflower, corn and soya bean. These fats lower the level of cholesterol in the blood.

puree: a smooth paste, usually of vegetables or fruits, made by putting foods through a sieve, food mill or liquefying in a blender or food processor.

ragout: traditionally a well-seasoned, rich stew containing meat, vegetables and wine. Nowadays, a term applied to any stewed mixture.

ramekins: small oval or round individual baking dishes.**reconstitute:** to put moisture back into dehydrated foods by soaking in liquid.

reduce: to cook over a very high heat, uncovered, until the liquid is reduced by evaporation.

refresh: to cool hot food quickly, either under running water or by plunging it into iced water, to stop it cooking. Particularly for vegetables and occasionally for shellfish.

rice vinegar: mild, fragrant vinegar that is less sweet than cider vinegar and not as harsh as distilled malt vinegar. Japanese rice vinegar is milder than the Chinese variety.

roulade: a piece of meat, usually pork or veal, that is spread with stuffing, rolled and often braised or poached. A roulade may also be a sweet or savoury mixture that is baked in a Swiss roll tin or paper case, filled with a contrasting filling, and rolled.

rubbing-in: a method of incorporating fat into flour, by use of fingertips only. Also incorporates air into mixture.

safflower oil: the vegetable oil that contains the highest proportion of polyunsaturated fats.

salsa: a juice derived from the main ingredient being cooked or a sauce added to a dish to enhance its flavour. In Italy the term is often used for pasta sauces; in Mexico the name usually applies to uncooked sauces served as an accompaniment, especially to corn chips.

saturated fats: one of the three types of fats found in foods. These exist in large quantities in animal products, coconut and palm oils; they raise the level of cholesterol in the blood. As high cholesterol levels may cause heart disease, saturated fat consumption is recommended to be less than 15% of kilojoules provided by the daily diet.

sauté: to cook or brown in small amount of hot fat.

score: to mark food with cuts, notches of lines to prevent curling or to make food more attractive.

scald: to bring just to boiling point, usually for milk. Also to rinse with boiling water.

sear: to brown surface quickly over high heat in hot dish.

seasoned flour: flour with salt and pepper added.

sift: to shake a dry, powdered substance through a sieve or sifter to remove any lumps and give lightness.

simmer: to cook food gently in liquid that bubbles steadily just below boiling point so that the food cooks in even heat without breaking up.

singe: to quickly flame poultry to remove all traces of feathers after plucking.

skim: to remove a surface layer (often of impurities and scum) from a liquid with a metal spoon or small ladle.

slivered: sliced in long, thin pieces, usually refers to nuts, especially almonds.

soften: re gelatine - sprinkle over cold water and allow to gel (soften) then dissolve and liquefy.

souse: to cover food, particularly fish, in wine vinegar and spices and cook slowly; the food is cooled in the same liquid. Sousing gives food a pickled flavour.

steep: to soak in warm or cold liquid in order to soften food and draw out strong flavours or impurities.

stir-fry: to cook thin slices of meat and vegetable over a high heat in a small amount of oil, stirring constantly to even cooking in a short time. Traditionally cooked in a wok, however a heavy based frying pan may be used.

stock: a liquid containing flavours, extracts and nutrients of bones, meat, fish or vegetables.

stud: to adorn with; for example, baked ham studded with whole cloves.

sweat: to cook vegetables over heat until only juices run.

sugo: an Italian sauce made from the liquid or juice extracted from fruit or meat during cooking.

sweat: to cook sliced or chopped food, usually vegetables, in a little fat and no liquid over very low heat. Foil is pressed on top so that the food steams in its own juices, usually before being added to other dishes.

timbale: a creamy mixture of vegetables or meat baked in a mould. French for "kettledrum"; also denotes a drum-shaped baking dish.

thicken: to make a thin, smooth paste by mixing together arrowroot, cornflour or flour with an equal amount of cold water; stir into hot liquid, cook, stirring until thickened.

toss: to gently mix ingredients with two forks or fork spoon.

total fat: the individual daily intake of all three fats previously described in this glossary. Nutritionists recommend that fats provide no more than 35% of the energy in the diet.

vine leaves: tender, lightly flavoured leaves of the grapevine, used in ethnic cuisine as wrappers for savoury mixtures. As the leaves are usually packed in brine, they should be well rinsed before use.

whip: to beat rapidly, incorporate air and produce expansion.

zest: thin outer layer of citrus fruits containing the aromatic citrus oil. It is usually thinly pared with a vegetable peeler, or grated with a zester or grater to separate it from the bitter white pith underneath.

INDEX

INDEX

FAVOURITE RECIPES

NOTES

NOTES